ESTHER
A MODERN COMMENTARY

Translation and Commentary by

LEONARD S. KRAVITZ
and
KERRY M. OLITZKY

URJ PRESS
NEW YORK, NEW YORK

For permission to reprint, please contact URJ Press at:

URJ Press
633 Third Avenue
New York, NY 10017–6778

(212) 650–4124
press@urj.org

Library of Congress Cataloging-in-Publication Data

Kravitz, Leonard S.
   Esther : a modern commentary / translation and commentary by Leonard S. Kravitz
And Kerry M. Olitzky.
     p. cm.
   Includes bibliographical references.
   ISBN 978-0-8074-1139-1
  1. Bible. O.T. Esther–Commentaries. I. Olitzky, Kerry M. II. Bible. O.T. Esther.
English. 2010. III. Title.
  BS1375.53.K73 2010
  222'.9077–dc22

                                              2009041488

Typesetting: El Ot Pre Press & Computing Ltd., Tel Aviv
Printed on acid-free paper
Copyright © 2010 by Leonard Kravitz and Kerry Olitzky
Manufactured in the United States of America

10 9 8 7 6 5 4 3 2 1

To Hannah,
as ever.
LSK

To Aliza Shoshana Olitzky
and Akiva Menachem Olitzky
representing the past
and taking us into the future.
KMO

Contents

Permissions

Every attempt has been made to obtain permission to reprint previously published material. The authors gratefully acknowledge the following for permission to reprint previously published material:

BARER LITERARY: "The Monica Metaphor" written by Lauren Grodstein, first printed in *The Modern Jewish Girl's Guide to Guilt*, edited by Ruth Andrew Ellenson © 2006. Used by permission of Barer Literary and Lauren Grodstein.

BEHRMAN HOUSE: Excerpt from *The Extraordinary Nature of Ordinary Things* by Steven Z. Leder © Behrman House., Inc., reprinted with permission. www.behrmanhouse.com.

GEFEN PUBLISHING HOUSE: Excerpt from *Roots of the Future* by Rabbi Herb Friedman, Gefen Publishing House Ltd. www.gefenpublishing.com.

INKWELL MANAGEMENT: Excerpt from *The Mask Jews Wear: The Self-Deception of American Jewry* by Eugene Borowitz © 1973. Used by permission of InkWell Management.

JERUSALEM REPORT: "The Amelek Dilemma" by David Ellenson, *The Jerusalem Report*, March 24, 2003.

JEWISH LIGHTS PUBLISHING: Excerpts from *Soul Judaism: Dancing with God into a New Era* by Wayne Dosick © 1999, *A Living Covenant: The Innovative Spirit in Traditional Judaism* by David Hartman © 1997, *The Spirit of Renewal: Crisis and Response in Jewish Life* by Edward Feld © 1991, *Invisible Lines of Connection: Sacred Stories of the Ordinary* by Lawrence Kushner © 1996, *The Sacred Art of Fasting* by Thomas Ryan © 2005, *Godwrestling: Round Two* by Arthur Waskow © 1996, *Restful Reflections: Nighttime Inspiration to Calm the Soul, Based on Jewish Wisdom* by Kerry M. Olitzky and Lori Forman © 2001. Permission granted by Jewish Lights Publishing, P.O. Box 237, Woodstock, VT 05091.

JEWISH PUBLICATION SOCIETY: Excerpt from *Engendering Judaism: An Inclusive Theology and Ethics* by Rachel Adler © 1998. Used by permission of the Jewish Publication Society.

Acknowledgments

This book is for the many adults, in particular, who abide by perennial Purim celebrations for the sake of our children—the Jewish future—forsaking a more mature observance of the holiday so that others may enjoy it.

We thank Rabbi Hara Person, former editor in chief of URJ Press, for helping us to navigate the process of bringing sacred writ to a liberal public, helping them to gain immediate access to the richness of our written tradition so that it might bring meaning to their personal religious lives. We also thank Michael Goldberg and the staff of the URJ Press, including Debra Hirsch Corman, Rebecca Rosenfeld, Stephen Becker, Victor Ney, Jessica Katz, Jonathan Levine, and Michael Silber, who have not wavered from supporting the journey to move this series forward. They are full partners in this process. With this publication, we will have succeeded in creating—among other texts—commentaries on all five *m'gillot*. Like Esther, all of the *m'gillot* that we have translated and annotated are designed to enhance a mature and liberal appreciation of the holiday with which it is associated, as well as of the sacred text itself.

For all those students who have given us the privilege of sharing our Torah with them, and for the blessing of being able to continue this sacred work together as friends and colleagues who move from one generation to another, we are grateful.

We thank our families for their unconditional support, without which none of this holy work would be possible.

Leonard S. Kravitz
Kerry ("Shia") Olitzky
Chanukah 5767

Introduction

The Book of Esther, usually referred to as *M'gillat Esther*, the Scroll of Esther, is a great story, so well-written that even critics of its historicity are impressed by its high level of engaging literary fiction. As part of the third section of the *Tanach* called the Writings (*K'tuvim*), it matters not whether Esther is fiction or embellished fact, since the essence of the story compels us to grapple with the issues it raises year after year. Like four other books in the Bible that are also known as "scrolls" (because they were originally attached to a single wooden roller—unlike the Torah, whose size requires two wooden rollers), the reading of *M'gillat Esther* is assigned to a particular holiday. In the case of Esther, it is read twice: on the evening and morning of Purim.

In Esther, the author has re-created the customs of the age of Xerxes (fifth century B.C.E.) and the idiosyncrasies of the ancient Persian monarch, which included a vast harem and long-lasting parties that were marked by an over-abundance of women, wine, food, and ribald entertainment. Yet, there are no extant texts that corroborate the existence of the main characters of the Esther story (Mordecai, Esther, Vashti, Haman), even if Ahasuerus is, in fact, King Xerxes. If we were to use the story and what we know about the reign of Xerxes, it would place Mordecai in the story at 120 years old (Esther 2:5–6). However, if we take note of the Bible's use of time as six-month agricultural periods rather than twelve-month years, as some scholars suggest, then the age of 60 is much more reasonable.

Some questions remain. For example, why did Purim retain a Persian name and not a Hebrew one? Many will say that the name comes from *pur* (lot), to designate the lots that Haman used to determine the day on which to execute the Jews. Such a name would imply that the book is more about chance and its role in human life than it is about faith or God or prayer, themes that we would expect in a book of the Bible. It seems that neither piety nor virtue carries the action forward in the book. Instead, chance does. Some scholars suggest that the *Purim* comes from *purah*, the Hebrew word for winepress. Still others believe that Purim celebrates the victory of Judah the Maccabee over the Assyrian general Nicanor in 161 B.C.E., although there is much evidence to dispute this theory.

It seems credible that there was an ancient Jewish community in Persia, but it doesn't seem quite as credible that the entire community would be put at risk because of the failure of one of its members to fulfill a matter of court etiquette. If we assume that the Book of Esther reports real events, then perhaps there is more to the story. Could it be that the report of an attempt on the king's life might have reflected some real event? If Haman offered a bribe to the king to have the Jews killed, is the report that the king assented but did not take the bribe credible? If Haman hated Jews, irrespective of the reason, would a king—married to a Jewish woman, albeit unknowingly—have hated them as well? Would the king indeed have made Mordecai, the leader of the Jews, his vizier?

All of the unanswered questions make the dating of the book somewhat difficult. According to the Rabbis of the Babylonian Talmud (*Bava Batra* 152a), it dates to the period of the Great Assembly, a historically questionable institution in its own right. Modern scholars often assign it to the Greek period (333–63 B.C.E.).

Much of the discussion concerning Purim and the Book of Esther is focused on the fact that God's name is never mentioned. (This is also the reason why many *sof'rim* [scribes] begin their serious work with the writing of a *m'gillah* rather than a Torah scroll.) But the notion of a hidden God is also a powerful theological statement.

According to contemporary theologian Rabbi Irving (Yitz) Greenberg, by placing the Book of Esther into the canon—despite a great deal of resistance—the people and the Rabbis showed that they understood how God acts in history in the post-prophetic age. They came to realize that God does not operate as a force that crashes into history from outside. Rather God is in the center of life, present in the natural and in the redemptive process in which the human is copartner. This comports with a more modern and liberal understanding of the place of God in our lives, in the world, and in the Book of Esther.

For the contemporary liberal Jewish community, the Purim story, however imperfect, seems to emerge from some experience that has compelled the Jewish people to celebrate it for so long. The facts may be embellished, but they do not seem to have been imagined or dreamed up. Given the experience of the Jewish people, especially in the last century, it takes no stretch of the imagination to envision the events that are recorded in the story. Too many people in too many places have risen up in an attempt to destroy us. *M'gillat Esther* may be described as historical fiction, but not as pure fiction, as some critics would have it. The Rabbis of the Jerusalem Talmud (1:8) say it best in the simplest of terms: "The Book of Esther will never lose its power." Perhaps this is one reason why they say elsewhere that while other holidays will cease to be celebrated during the messianic era, only the celebration of Purim will remain (*Midrash Mishlei* 9:2).

Unlike most other stories found in the Bible, the Book of Esther depends on chance to move the action forward, not divine intervention. Vashti's refusal to dance in front of Ahasuerus and his drunken friends leads to her banishment from the kingdom and an edict that women must obey the orders of their husbands. Then Esther vies to become queen (that is, the number-one harem girl), which in religious school and synagogue contexts is often translated as a beauty contest. Esther becoming queen, then, is the result of chance. Mordecai overhears a plot to overthrow the king and shares the information with Esther—a chance encounter.

For the liberal Jew, the challenge of Esther is how to take a story whose grounding in history is questionable and whose context for celebration is marked by its ribald frivolity, not to mention its focus on the consumption of alcohol, and make it spiritually meaningful. Most Purim celebrations (costume parades and carnivals) are designed for children, yet the Purim story and its inherent challenges are really very adult. The text of Esther itself, as will be demonstrated in this volume, is full of sexual nuance and innuendo, particularly designed for the attuned adult ear. Nevertheless, there are important questions to ponder. To what extent must one be willing to go in order to protect one's personal dignity? How much compromise is permitted in order to save one's people? Can one use one's body for the benefit of saving lives? How should one deal with one's enemies, especially when one is powerful or victorious? Is the exacting of revenge acceptable, and if so, to what extent? Should we celebrate the demise of our enemies? These are important questions that, when contextualized in the ritual and worship environment, can directly impact our spiritual lives.

It is also important to note the various customs related to the reading of the *M'gillah*, since these customs provide us insight into its understanding, as well as how the Jewish people viewed the various messages in the Book of Esther throughout history. An entire Talmudic tractate that bears its name is dedicated to these rules and regulations. The Book of Esther has its own cantillation, thus setting it apart from the other books of the Bible, including the Torah and haftarah when they are read publicly. While the *M'gillah* is treated with a reverence similar to that reserved for the Torah scroll, *m'gillot* that are privately held and used in the presence of family (a common practice) are often lavishly embellished with illustrations. The obligation of reading applies to both men and women and can be fulfilled by listening to the reading rather than actually doing the reading itself.

Many readers are familiar with the reading of *M'gillat Esther* during Purim services. They are usually raucous and intentionally irreverent, as is much of the Purim celebration. Many of the customs of Purim observance turn the remainder of the year's customs on their head. For example, most holidays start with a celebratory meal; Purim ends with a feast. According to the Babylonian Talmud (*M'gillah* 14a), the reading of the *M'gillah* replaces the reading of *Hallel* (Psalms 113–118), commonly read at other festivals, which notes the deliverance of the Jewish people.

The *M'gillah* should be read while one is standing up, and directly from the scroll rather than by memory. During the reading, there are four special verses, called "verses of redemption" (*p'sukei g'ulah*), which are traditionally first said aloud by the congregation and then repeated by the reader (Esther 2:5, 8:15–16, 10:3). At certain key points in the Book of Esther (Esther 1:22, 2:4, 2:17, 4:14,

5:4, 6:1), it is customary for the reader to raise his or her voice. This adds drama to the story and, much like some of the elements in the Passover seder, is designed to maintain the attention of the children as well as the adults. According to Esther 6:1, which is the turning point in the story, the king cannot sleep and directs his servants to read the book of records of the chronicles to him. This verse is read very loudly, and some even apply a different melody to it since it signals the beginning of Israel's redemption in the story. An additional four verses enumerate the ten sons of Haman. These verses (Esther 9:6–10) are chanted in one breath in order to emphasize that the sons died together. This custom of chanting in one breath is already included in the Babylonian Talmud (*M'gillah* 16b). Another reason for this particular custom is that we are told to avoid giving the appearance that we are gloating over their fate. While not quite as nice, it might also be said that we don't want to waste our breath on them. These verses also appear in the *M'gillah* in a single column to signify the fact that Haman's sons were hanged on a single gallows, one on top of another. The peculiar Hebrew word "et," which precedes each of the sons' names, ends in the letter *tav*, the last letter of the Hebrew alphabet. From the repetition of this word we learn that Haman's sons will have no hope for the future.

Ideally, the reading of the *M'gillah* should take place in the presence of a minyan in the synagogue. Even if one can gather the requisite number in one's home, it is still preferable to go to the synagogue for the *M'gillah* reading, since, as Proverbs 14:28 reminds us, "The Sovereign's Glory is [made manifest] in the multitude." Since one of the reasons that we read the *M'gillah* is to publicize the miracles of Purim, this is best accomplished when it is read publicly in the synagogue. It is also interesting to note that the reading of the *M'gillah* takes precedence over the performance of all positive Torah precepts. Even the study of Torah is suspended so that people can hear the reading of the *M'gillah*. The only mitzvah that we do not suspend for the reading of the *M'gillah* is the mitzvah of providing burial for a person who has no one else to bury him.

It is customary to spread out the entire *M'gillah* on the reading table rather than keeping it rolled like a Torah. But the sheets of the *M'gillah* are folded like a letter so that the parchment does not fall to the ground. This treatment emerges from Esther 9:29, which refers to the *M'gillah* as a letter.

As people continued to grapple with the meaning of the Book of Esther—as is the case with the remainder of Jewish literature—a library of literature called "commentary" grew around it. Commentaries were written as each generation sought to view this story through the lens of its own time and understanding. To read a sacred text is to bring oneself to the ideas of another time and place. Each generation's attempt to understand a particular text provides a foundation for the succeeding generation to do the same. In this volume, we primarily view the text through the lenses of three different commentators: the author(s) of the *Targum*, a circa fifth-century Aramaic translation, interpretation, and commentary on the Hebrew text; Rashi (1040–1105); and Abraham ibn Ezra (1092–1167). Since the *Targum* and Rashi (perhaps Judaism's commentator par excellence because of his encyclopedic sweep of classic Jewish text and tradition) reflect the notions of Rabbinic Judaism, their interpretations share a lot in common. Rashi also attempted to ascertain the literal or contextual meaning of the text. What is unique about the *Targum* is that while it purports only to be a translation into Aramaic (a sister language of Hebrew and the spoken language of Jews of the time), it is really as much interpretation and pedagogical tool as translation, especially since the *Targum* was frequently read aloud in Aramaic as the Bible (more often the Torah) was being read in public. A minor tractate of the Talmud, *Sof'rim* (literally, "Scribes"), attributes the Aramaic translation of Esther to a Rabbi Joseph (*Sof'rim* 8, Rule 5). While it is not clear whether Rabbi Joseph was, in fact, the composer of this Aramaic translation, the *Targum* certainly reads Esther through the lens of Rabbinic Judaism, as will be seen from the commentary on it. The remarks made by Ibn Ezra—who wrote his commentaries in Rome, Mantua, and London—on the other hand, reflect the impact of Greek philosophy on Judaism. He sought to bring a critical, almost modern, approach to his interpretation of the text. Ibn Ezra favored the plain sense of the text over traditional interpretations and was one of the forerunners of biblical criticism. His insights are also very helpful in understanding the classic positions of medieval Jewish philosophy. On occasion, we also take guidance from the *Biblia Hebraica*, a familiar critical edition of the Bible edited by Kittel. Finally, we take some direction from the critical scholarly work of Ludwig Koehler and Walter Baumgartner and regularly consult their *Lexicon* as a reference. We read these various commentaries along with Esther to see whether earlier understandings might illumine the text for us. As each of their worlds formed the lens through which they read the text, so the world in which we live may form the lens through which we read the text. The mini-essays found at the end of each chapter elucidate various facts and figures that emerge either in the text itself or in the commentary. Similarly, gleanings found following the mini-essays present other voices—more contemporary—that add their own insights to the themes that are implicit in the chapter under discussion. By considering the views of others, we become more aware of how we form our own personal understanding of the text and consider the role it plays in our own spiritual lives.

CHAPTER ONE

א:א וַיְהִי בִּימֵי אֲחַשְׁוֵרוֹשׁ הוּא אֲחַשְׁוֵרוֹשׁ הַמֹּלֵךְ מֵהֹדּוּ וְעַד־כּוּשׁ
שֶׁבַע וְעֶשְׂרִים וּמֵאָה מְדִינָה:

1:1 THIS HAPPENED IN THE TIME OF AHASUERUS, THE SAME
AHASUERUS WHO RULED FROM INDIA TO ETHIOPIA,
127 PROVINCES IN ALL.

This verse introduces the Book of Esther and offers the reader a context for the events
that follow. The narrator assumes that the reader is familiar with a king named
Ahasuerus, who ruled an extensive territory representing the ancient Persian kingdom,
including present-day Iran, the story's setting. The *Targum* expands the king's
biography by suggesting that he lived at the time of the destruction of the First Temple
in Jerusalem, "when worship ceased at the House of our God." To help the reader
place the story in further historical context, the *Targum* adds that such worship ceased
until the second year of the reign of the Persian king Darius. Wanting to provide the
reader with even more of an introduction, the *Targum* anticipates the action of the
story—and reveals its opinion of at least one of the characters in the story—telling
readers that the reason worship stopped and the Temple was not rebuilt "was
because of the evil advice given by the wicked Vashti, daughter of Evil-Merodach son
of Nebuchadnezzar [who was the Babylonian king]." The punishment for that
advice—something of which most readers are not aware—was "that it was decreed
that she would be executed naked." Because he accepted her advice, Nebuchadnezzar's life was shortened, his kingdom was divided, and the nations and peoples
who previously obeyed him no longer did so. Because of Vashti's "sin," Esther would
be raised to the role of queen, and she would rule over 127 provinces.

The *Targum* notes that the introduction of the verse *vay'hi bimei* (literally, "It came
to pass in the days of"), which we translate as "This happened in the time," suggests

1

a "time of suffering" and cites examples: "It came to pass in the time of Amraphel" (Genesis 14:1)—until that time there had been no war; "In the days when the judges governed, there was a famine in the land" (Ruth 1:1); "It came to pass in the days of Ahaz...that Rezin, king of Aram, marched up against Jerusalem" (Isaiah 7:1), "saying, 'Let us go up against Judah; let us tear it apart and divide it'" (Isaiah 7:5–6). Thus, the *Targum* explains that this phrase implies a disaster. However, the *Targum* notes a way to avoid the impending disaster: whenever a disaster strikes the House of Israel, if they pray to their Parent in heaven, God will answer them, as it is written, "And it shall come to pass that before they call, I will answer. And while they are speaking, I will hear" (Isaiah 65:24).

Rashi suggests that the first verse identifies Ahasuerus as the king of Persia who reigned in place of Cyrus at the end of the seventy years of the Babylonian exile. Rashi also understands the phrase "the same Ahasuerus" as a reference not to a specific person but rather to a particular personality trait. For him, the phrase "the same Ahasuerus" indicates that Ahasuerus remained the same wicked person from the beginning of his life until its end. Rashi reasons that since the verse identifies Ahasuerus as king, it is not necessary to add "who ruled." Therefore, this phrase indicates that Ahasuerus was not of royal lineage. Instead, he took the right to rule by force. Finally, Rashi is intrigued by the breadth of his kingdom. Referencing I Kings 5:4, Rashi suggests that the use of language in the phrase "from India to Ethiopia" indicates power. In this case, it suggests that Ahasuerus exerted such control over his dominions that it was as if India were next to Ethiopia.

It is Ibn Ezra's custom to begin his commentary with a poem. In the case of Esther, the poem praises God. Ibn Ezra takes the opportunity to note that the Book of Esther does not mention the Deity. Anticipating criticism, Ibn Ezra rejects the notion held by some teachers that the phrase *mimakom acheir* (literally, "from another place" [Esther 4:14]) in Mordecai's speech to Esther uses the euphemism *HaMakom* (literally, "the Place") as a reference to God. He is able to make this claim because *HaMakom* as a name for God is not found anywhere else in Scripture; rather, it is a Rabbinic invention. Moreover, if it were to refer to God, what meaning would the term *acheir*, "another" or "other," have? Ibn Ezra concludes that Mordecai wrote the Book of Esther and distributed copies of it (Esther 9:20). Since those who followed pagan gods included the name of their deity in their writings, Ibn Ezra reads the Book of Esther and the conspicuous absence of God's name in it as a tribute to the God of Israel.

While Ibn Ezra believes that the reader needs to know the precise time period referenced in this verse and the exact identity of the king who is called Ahasuerus, he disagrees with Rashi. Ibn Ezra (incorrectly) claims that Ahasuerus was the king who ruled after Cyrus and Zerubbabel following the destruction of the Second Temple. But the Temple had not yet been built. He thinks that Ahasuerus is the Artaxerxes mentioned in the Book of Ezra (4:7) and interprets *vay'hi bimei* simply as a literary figure of speech that indicates the beginning of a story. For Ibn Ezra, the phrase "the same Ahasuerus" may suggest that there might have been another king with the same name who ruled in another area that was located between India and Ethiopia.

א:ב בַּיָּמִים הָהֵם כְּשֶׁבֶת הַמֶּלֶךְ אֲחַשְׁוֵרוֹשׁ עַל כִּסֵּא מַלְכוּתוֹ אֲשֶׁר בְּשׁוּשַׁן הַבִּירָה:

1:2 In those days, King Ahasuerus occupied the throne in the fortified city of Shushan.

Seeking to understand the peculiar way that the Hebrew is phrased at the beginning of the verse (literally, "in those days, like sitting"), Rashi explains *k'shevet* ("like sitting," which we translate as "occupied") to refer to the establishment of Ahasuerus's reign. In other words, he had just taken over as king. This reference originally comes from the Babylonian Talmud, *M'gillah* 11b. In contrast, Ibn Ezra suggests that *k'shevet* is a reference to the period after Ahasuerus had paused from involvement in wars dealing with India and Ethiopia. He explains *habirah*, "the fortified city," as "the palace."

The *Targum* takes the reference to the throne quite literally, telling the story of the physical chair on which Ahasuerus sat. It traces the origin of King Ahasuerus's throne to Solomon, claiming that the throne was taken from Jerusalem by Shishak, king of Egypt. From Egypt, it was taken by Sennacherib, but Hezekiah took it back from Sennacherib and returned it to Jerusalem. It was removed from Jerusalem once again by Pharaoh Hagirah, king of Egypt. Then Nebuchadnezzar took it from Hagirah and brought it with him to Babylon. When Cyrus conquered Median Babylon, he brought it down to Elam. Next, Ahasuerus reigned. According to the *Targum*, he wanted to sit on the throne, but he was reticent to do so since he didn't think it looked like Solomon's throne. So Ahasuerus brought artisans from Alexandria to make one like it, but they were unable to do so. Others were able to fashion a base, but it took them two years. It wasn't until the third year of his reign that Ahasuerus was able to sit on the copy of Solomon's throne that the artisans made in the fortified city of Shushan.

אָ:ג בִּשְׁנַת שָׁלוֹשׁ לְמָלְכוֹ עָשָׂה מִשְׁתֶּה לְכָל־שָׂרָיו וַעֲבָדָיו חֵיל פָּרַס וּמָדַי הַפַּרְתְּמִים וְשָׂרֵי הַמְּדִינוֹת לְפָנָיו:

1:3 IN THE THIRD YEAR OF HIS REIGN, HE GAVE A BANQUET FOR ALL: HIS PRINCES AND COURTIERS, THE OFFICERS OF THE ARMY OF PERSIA AND MEDIA, THE NOBLES AND THE PROVINCIAL GOVERNORS WERE ALL PRESENT.

While this verse reads like a guest list for Ahasuerus's party, it also reveals the structure of the court of Ahasuerus. Nevertheless, the roles of the ranks as presented by the author are unclear. Partially following Koehler-Baumgartner (p. 311), we translate *cheil Paras uMadai* as "the officers of the army of Persia and Media," feeling that its translation of "army, armed forces" does not precisely or accurately fit this context. We also follow Koehler-Baumgartner (p. 979) in our translation of *part'mim* as "nobles." Rashi chooses to translate the word as "rulers."

In an attempt to explain who attended the party, what their roles were, and what they were doing there in the first place, the *Targum* uses its translation to suggest that some (unnamed people) believed that Ahasuerus's party caused some of the pro-vincial officers to rebel against him. Ahasuerus was thereby forced to wage war against them. Having conquered them, he threw another party. According to the *Targum*, some say that it was a particular pagan holy day that Ahasuerus proclaimed, ordering that the officials of the province appear before him to rejoice. So 127 kings from 127 provinces came to the banquet with crowns on their heads. Resting on precious wool, they ate and rejoiced with the king. Nobles from various provinces also attended. There were even some officials of the people of Israel, who were there to bewail the vessels of the Temple that had been brought to Persia.

Still looking for the reason why Ahasuerus prepared a banquet for his court, Ibn Ezra writes that some say that he did so because his calculations indicated that Israel would not be redeemed, others that the party marked the end of Ahasuerus's wars, and still others (and this is the view with which Ibn Ezra agrees) that the banquet was given because Ahasuerus had just married Vashti. Accordingly, Ibn Ezra translates *part'mim* as "belonging to the royal family," a word found only in the Books of Esther and Daniel.

א:ד בְּהַרְאֹתוֹ אֶת־עֹשֶׁר כְּבוֹד מַלְכוּתוֹ וְאֶת־יְקָר תִּפְאֶרֶת גְּדוּלָּתוֹ יָמִים רַבִּים שְׁמוֹנִים וּמְאַת יוֹם:

1:4 FOR ALL OF 180 DAYS, HE SHOWED OFF THE GREAT WEALTH OF HIS KINGDOM AND THE MAGNIFICENT GLORY OF HIS POWER.

Ahasuerus is a showman and braggart, a rather usual posture for a king of his ilk. In this verse, the author emphasizes the extent of Ahasuerus's wealth. The *Targum* expands the verse in its translation, emphasizing the reason for the length of the party as well: "After eating, drinking, and indulging themselves, they [the invited guests] were shown the wealth that he [Ahasuerus] had retained when he conquered Cyrus, who had acquired his wealth by conquering Babylonia. Digging in a Persian district, he found 680 brass vessels filled with gold, as well as gems of various kinds including emeralds and onyx. That show of wealth made for glory, astounding the nobles for 180 days."

א:ה וּבִמְלוֹאת הַיָּמִים הָאֵלֶּה עָשָׂה הַמֶּלֶךְ לְכָל־הָעָם הַנִּמְצְאִים בְּשׁוּשַׁן הַבִּירָה לְמִגָּדוֹל וְעַד־קָטָן מִשְׁתֶּה שִׁבְעַת יָמִים בַּחֲצַר גִּנַּת בִּיתַן הַמֶּלֶךְ:

1:5 AT THE END OF THESE DAYS, THE KING THEN GAVE ANOTHER BANQUET IN THE GARDEN OF THE PALACE FOR EVERYONE IN THE FORTRESS OF SHUSHAN, FROM THE LEAST TO THE GREATEST.

The partying was insufficient for the king, and so he parties on. In this case, the guest list is extended beyond the elite of the kingdom. We follow Koehler-Baumgartner (pp. 199, 129) in our translation of the unfamiliar words *ginat bitan* as "the garden of the palace." Rashi tells us that such a location is "a place with lush greens planted with trees." For clarity, we add "another" in our translation. It seems that the author wants to emphasize the "party nature" of this particular king. Nevertheless, Ibn Ezra argues that the phrase "everyone in the fortress" indicates that the entire array of officials is present; this would leave the common folk uninvited.

Wondering whether Persian Jews are invited to this second banquet, the *Targum* suggests that the banquet is for those Jews who are willing to live among those who are not circumcised—the citizens of Persia—and therefore "unworthy" of being invited according to the *Targum*. Following a description of the ornate furnishings of the garden, the *Targum* makes sure that the reader realizes that Mordecai and his associates are not present at the party.

א:ו חוּר כַּרְפַּס וּתְכֵלֶת אָחוּז בְּחַבְלֵי־בוּץ וְאַרְגָּמָן עַל־גְּלִילֵי כֶסֶף וְעַמּוּדֵי שֵׁשׁ מִטּוֹת זָהָב וָכֶסֶף עַל רִצְפַת בַּהַט־וָשֵׁשׁ וְדַר וְסֹחָרֶת:

1:6 IN THE GARDEN WERE CURTAINS OF WHITE LINEN AND BLUE WOOL HELD UP BY CORDS OF WHITE BYSSUS AND RED PURPLE WOOL ATTACHED TO GOLDEN RINGS AND MARBLE COLUMNS, COUCHES OF SILVER AND GOLD UPON A FLOOR OF PRECIOUS STONES AND MARBLE, MOTHER OF PEARL AND BLACK MINERAL.

While the description is difficult to translate, it is obviously an ornate environment with garish furnishings. Our translation of the first three words in the verse (*chur, karpas, t'cheilet*) follows Koehler-Baumgartner (pp. 299, 500, and 1733). Our translation of the next words (*butz* and *argaman*) also follows Koehler-Baumgartner (pp. 115, 84), as does the translation of *b'hat, dar,* and *socharet* (pp. 111, 230, 750). The reader of Koehler-Baumgartner will note the tentative nature of all of these identifications. Regardless of the specific materials under discussion, they are expensive and their mention is employed to impress the reader with the extensive wealth of King Ahasuerus.

Rashi has a different sense of the furnishings. He takes the different colors mentioned by the author to refer to different materials used for the mattresses on the dining couches rather than as "curtains." Although not at all explicit in the text, Rashi understands the hangings to have been made of embroidered material. He thinks that "couches of silver and gold" were arranged for the banquet and that the "floor" was inset with precious stones. While the commentators—including the authors of this volume—disagree on the specific nature of the furnishings, all agree that they have one intended purpose: to demonstrate the extensive wealth of King Ahasuerus.

Also trying to understand the purpose of the extensive description and to connect the verses, Ibn Ezra explains the colors as follows: he derives *chur* as "white" from Aramaic and Arabic and *karpas* as "off-white." It is well-known that *t'cheilet* is "blue." Ibn Ezra thinks that silk was the material that was colored and takes *butz* to mean "linen." For him, the "golden rings" were set between the "columns" and, like Rashi, he speculates that the floor was decorated with inset precious stones.

אז וְהַשְׁקוֹת בִּכְלֵי זָהָב וְכֵלִים מִכֵּלִים שׁוֹנִים וְיֵין מַלְכוּת רָב כְּיַד הַמֶּלֶךְ:

1:7 AT THE KING'S PLEASURE, VAST AMOUNTS OF ROYAL WINE WERE SERVED IN GOLDEN GOBLETS OF VARIOUS KINDS.

Where did these goblets come from, and what is special about royal wine? wonder some of the commentators—as if this verse were not simply a further description of the nature of the party and of the king's extensive wealth. For traditional commentators, the Book of Esther, like the rest of the Bible, is sacred writ, so every word, phrase, and verse expresses an important notion. It is the reader's obligation to discern it. So the *Targum* identifies the "golden goblets" as those taken by Nebuchadnezzar from Jerusalem, as well as many others that Ahasuerus already owned.

Rashi shares with readers a story that Ahasuerus provided each individual with wine that had been made before that person was born. He explains *mikeilim shonim* (which we translate as "goblets of various kinds") as "goblets strange in appearance."

Ibn Ezra explains *k'yad hamelech* (here translated as "at the king's pleasure") as "in accordance with the king's power." Like Rashi, Ibn Ezra thinks that *shonim* has a stronger meaning than "various," taking it to mean "very different."

א:ח וְהַשְׁתִיָּה כַדָּת אֵין אֹנֵס כִּי־כֵן יִסַּד הַמֶּלֶךְ עַל כָּל־רַב בֵּיתוֹ
לַעֲשׂוֹת כִּרְצוֹן אִישׁ־וָאִישׁ:

**1:8 THE DRINKING FOLLOWED THE RULE: "NO RULES!"
THE KING HAD ORDERED EVERY WINE STEWARD TO
PROVIDE FOR EVERY GUEST WHATEVER HE WANTED.**

The author clearly wants to convey to the reader the ribald nature of Ahasuerus's party. The result of free-flowing wine is usually drunkenness and the drunken behavior that follows. The phrase *ein oneis* is difficult to render in idiomatic English. The words might be translated literally as "no force." The context suggests that the sense of the phrase is that each drinker could drink as he wished without anyone forcing him to change his pattern of drinking. Hence, it seems that the closest idiomatic translation is "No rules!"

The *Targum* distinguishes between the Jews and non-Jews at the king's party, translating "whatever he wanted" as "the will of each Jew [*bar Yisrael*] and every non-Jew [*min kol umah v'lishan*]."

Perhaps wanting us to understand the social pressure felt by those who attended the king's banquets, Rashi claims that there are some parties and banquets at which the guests are compelled to drink a great deal whether or not they want to do so. He explains *kol rav beito*, which we translate as "every wine steward," as "master of the banquet" and specifies them as "the chief bakers, the chief cooks, and the chief butlers."

א:ט גַּם וַשְׁתִּי הַמַּלְכָּה עָשְׂתָה מִשְׁתֵּה נָשִׁים בֵּית הַמַּלְכוּת אֲשֶׁר
לַמֶּלֶךְ אֲחַשְׁוֵרוֹשׁ:

**1:9 VASHTI ALSO GAVE A BANQUET FOR WOMEN IN THE
ROYAL PALACE OF AHASUERUS.**

The author wants the reader to understand that the king's banquet is for men only, except for those women who might be asked to serve and entertain them. In addition, there is a banquet for elite women, but the exact nature of that banquet is not stated.

However, the *Targum*, in its translation, tells us that the women's banquet takes place in Vashti's bedroom.

אֵי בַּיּוֹם הַשְּׁבִיעִי כְּטוֹב לֵב־הַמֶּלֶךְ בַּיָּיִן אָמַר לִמְהוּמָן בִּזְּתָא חַרְבוֹנָא בִּגְתָא וַאֲבַגְתָא זֵתַר וְכַרְכַּס שִׁבְעַת הַסָּרִיסִים הַמְשָׁרְתִים אֶת־פְּנֵי הַמֶּלֶךְ אֲחַשְׁוֵרוֹשׁ:

1:10 ON THE SEVENTH DAY, WHEN THE KING WAS FEELING REALLY GOOD BECAUSE OF THE WINE, HE ORDERED THE SEVEN EUNUCHS WHO SERVED HIM, MEHUMAN, BIZZETHA, HARBONA, BIGTHA, ABAGTHA, ZETHAR, AND CARCAS,

The picture is clear. Ahasuerus is drunk, the result of seven days of drinking. Although he is intoxicated, he retains the power as the king to order others to do what he wants. As we see in the next verse—which is coupled with this verse—he orders his wife to come forth and display her beauty.

This is not an acceptable image for the *Targum*, so it chooses to change the message in its translation: "The righteous Mordecai prayed to God from the first day of the banquet to the seventh day, which was the Sabbath, eating no bread and drinking no water. On the Sabbath day, he entered before him [the king] and before the Sanhedrin in the presence of God. When the heart of the king was merry with wine, God sent the angel of incitement to disturb the banquet so that he [the king] would order Mehuman, Bizzetha, Harbona, Bigtha, Abagtha, Zethar, and Carcas...." The *Targum* continues by providing folk etymologies for each of the eunuchs. These names all point to the punishment that they will endure as a result of their service to the king. Mehuman was appointed to provide *mehumta*, "confusion." Bizzetha is *buz beita*, "a shame for the house." Harbona, *achar beih*, is "to be behind him." Bigtha and Abagtha are "in the future, the Master of the universe will squeeze them like a person squeezes grapes twice into a vat." God will in the future hunt and deal with these seven wicked lords who serve the wicked King Ahasuerus. Ibn Ezra, noting that the names are Persian, rejects the meanings of the names as suggested by the *Targum*.

It is interesting to note that some Hebrew linguists believe that the word for eunuch, *saris*, an Assyrian loan word, is used because when written in Hebrew characters (סריס) it actually looks like what it is intended to describe.

אַ:יא לְהָבִיא אֶת־וַשְׁתִּי הַמַּלְכָּה לִפְנֵי הַמֶּלֶךְ בְּכֶתֶר מַלְכוּת לְהַרְאוֹת
הָעַמִּים וְהַשָּׂרִים אֶת־יָפְיָהּ כִּי־טוֹבַת מַרְאֶה הִיא:

1:11 To bring Vashti the queen before the king wearing the royal crown to display her beauty to the people and to the princes, for she was indeed beautiful.

What happens to Vashti helps to establish the plot for the rest of the story. It is unclear but certainly intimated that the king orders Vashti to come wearing perhaps only the crown and nothing else. The *Targum* assumes such an interpretation and attributes it to Vashti's moral breakdown. According to the *Targum*, "The king ordered seven courtiers to bring Vashti the Queen naked. This was [punishment] for her having made Jewish girls work naked cording wool and flax on the Sabbath. Because of this, it was decreed against her to be brought naked, dressed only in her royal crown on her head."

Ibn Ezra thinks that the showing of a woman's beauty might have been the pattern of the land of Edom, that is, Europe. He expresses the opinion that Vashti's refusal to appear before the king (v. 12) might be due to her stemming from a people whose custom was that women conceal themselves in clothing. He also suggests something rather obvious: perhaps she refuses because she knows that her husband is drunk.

א:יב וַתְּמָאֵן הַמַּלְכָּה וַשְׁתִּי לָבוֹא בִּדְבַר הַמֶּלֶךְ אֲשֶׁר בְּיַד הַסָּרִיסִים
וַיִּקְצֹף הַמֶּלֶךְ מְאֹד וַחֲמָתוֹ בָּעֲרָה בוֹ:

1:12 ALTHOUGH THE KING'S ORDER HAD BEEN DELIVERED
BY THE EUNUCHS, QUEEN VASHTI REFUSED TO COME.
THE KING BECAME FURIOUS; HE WAS CONSUMED WITH
ANGER.

The king is angry because Vashti refuses his direct order. But he is exceptionally angry because her refusal is a public act of insubordination. Not only do the eunuchs know about her refusal, but so would all whom they would tell.

Rashi does not believe that Vashti's refusal is a result of her modesty. He quotes a Rabbinic statement (Babylonian Talmud, *M'gillah* 12b) suggesting that Vashti has a sudden onset of leprosy.

א:יג וַיֹּאמֶר הַמֶּלֶךְ לַחֲכָמִים יֹדְעֵי הָעִתִּים כִּי־כֵן דְּבַר הַמֶּלֶךְ לִפְנֵי
כָּל־יֹדְעֵי דָת וָדִין:

1:13 THE KING SPOKE TO THOSE SCHOLARY ADVISORS WHO
KNEW THE TIMES OF JUDGMENT, FOR THE KING'S WORD
CAME BEFORE THOSE WHO KNEW PRINCIPLES AND
PRECEDENTS OF LAW.

After Vashti's act of defiance, the king consults his advisors. Nevertheless, this is a difficult verse to translate and interpret. The word *itim* is the plural of *eit*, "time." It is unclear what "the times" would mean and what "the scholarly advisors who knew the times" would know. Koehler-Baumgartner (p. 901), whom we follow in the translation of this verse, suggests the times as "times of judgment." *Dat* can be either "order" or "law." Since it is not clear, we propose translating it as "principles and precedents of law."

The *Targum* tells us that these legal experts are the sons of Issachar, who were wise in the science of the times and seasons in the Torah, as well as the astrological calculations that would determine when it would be fitting for the king's word to be proclaimed before every scholar of the Torah and the law. (It would, of course, be unlikely that the king would hire Jewish scholars or that they would work for him in the first place, but the *Targum* offers this explanation because it sees the Torah and Judaism as central to the world.)

Rashi explains that *d'var hamelech* (the king's word) means that it was the king's practice to place every matter of judgment before a group of scholars. Ibn Ezra tells us that these "scholars of the times" are either astronomers or historians who know what previous kings have done (in similar circumstances).

א:יד וְהַקָּרֹב אֵלָיו כַּרְשְׁנָא שֵׁתָר אַדְמָתָא תַרְשִׁישׁ מֶרֶס מַרְסְנָא מְמוּכָן שִׁבְעַת שָׂרֵי פָּרַס וּמָדַי רֹאֵי פְּנֵי הַמֶּלֶךְ הַיּשְׁבִים רִאשֹׁנָה בַּמַּלְכוּת:

1:14 Carshena, Shethar, Admatha, Tarshish, Meres, Marsena, and Memucan were the seven princes closest to the king. They were admitted to the royal presence, and they occupied the highest rank in the kingdom.

In this verse, the author tells us a little more about the advisors mentioned in the previous verse. Returning to the notion that they are the sons of Issachar, the *Targum* claims that they are unwilling to make a judgment. It seems that they prayed to God and asked God that the banquet be interrupted so that the righteous persons who had offered sacrifices of one-year-old rams and two doves in the Temple by the hand of the High Priest and garbed in the breastplate and who had mingled the blood to make the bread of display would be remembered. However, when the king takes his place among the seven named princes, he asks their advice.

Rashi claims that the king presents his views before the seven princes (in order to solicit their opinion and advice). Ibn Ezra tells us that the phrase *ro-ei p'nei hamelech* (admitted to the royal presence) suggests that there might have been some in the king's retinue who were not so admitted. That is why the verse is so specific about this group of princes.

א:טו כְּדָת מַה־לַעֲשׂוֹת בַּמַּלְכָּה וַשְׁתִּי עַל אֲשֶׁר לֹא־עָשְׂתָה אֶת־מַאֲמַר הַמֶּלֶךְ אֲחַשְׁוֵרוֹשׁ בְּיַד הַסָּרִיסִים:

1:15 [THE KING ASKED,] "ACCORDING TO THE LAW, WHAT SHOULD BE DONE TO VASHTI THE QUEEN FOR NOT OBEYING THE ORDER OF KING AHASUERUS CONVEYED BY THE EUNICHS?"

Perhaps the author is trying to offer a more sympathetic picture of a king who is simply trying to fulfill the obligations of the law, as if he has no choice. Or maybe the king is truly at a loss and wants to know what the law calls for in this situation.

א:טז וַיֹּאמֶר מְמוּכָן לִפְנֵי הַמֶּלֶךְ וְהַשָּׂרִים לֹא עַל־הַמֶּלֶךְ לְבַדּוֹ עָוְתָה וַשְׁתִּי הַמַּלְכָּה כִּי עַל־כָּל־הַשָּׂרִים וְעַל־כָּל־הָעַמִּים אֲשֶׁר בְּכָל־מְדִינוֹת הַמֶּלֶךְ אֲחַשְׁוֵרוֹשׁ:

1:16 MEMUCAN DECLARED IN THE PRESENCE OF THE KING AND THE PRINCES, "NOT ONLY DID QUEEN VASHTI WRONG THE KING BUT ALSO ALL OF THE PRINCES AND ALL OF THE PEOPLES IN THE PROVINCES OF KING AHASUERUS.

The author explains to the reader why Vashti's action is considered so egregious, anticipating why her punishment will be equally severe. This ensures that the reader knows that Vashti's transgression is not merely a response to a drunken king's whim. It is critical to the plot development for the entire Book of Esther. Apparently, Vashti must be supplanted because what she did touched the entire kingdom.

The *Targum* provides the reader with an unexpected surprise: it identifies Memucan as Haman in an otherwise literal translation of the verse.

אː‏יז כִּי־יֵצֵא דְבַר־הַמַּלְכָּה עַל־כָּל־הַנָּשִׁים לְהַבְזוֹת בַּעְלֵיהֶן בְּעֵינֵיהֶן
בְּאָמְרָם הַמֶּלֶךְ אֲחַשְׁוֵרוֹשׁ אָמַר לְהָבִיא אֶת־וַשְׁתִּי הַמַּלְכָּה לְפָנָיו
וְלֹא־בָאָה:

1:17 "THE EXAMPLE OF THE QUEEN WILL CAUSE ALL THE
WOMEN TO TREAT THEIR HUSBANDS WITH CONTEMPT,
FOR THEY WILL TALK ABOUT KING AHASUERUS OR-
DERING VASHTI THE QUEEN TO BE BROUGHT BEFORE
HIM AND HER NOT COMING.

Memucan's response is not inconsistent with some modern reactions to feminism.
The act of refusal by the First Wife of the kingdom is taken as the first step toward a
general breakdown of the established social order. While the modern reader may not
expect a spouse to assent to such an order by a drunken husband—and should
expect the queen to do no less—what we have learned about domestic violence
teaches us that this is a more nuanced situation. Some women certainly would refuse,
but given the imbalance between male and female power, especially in the ancient
world, Vashti's refusal is particularly brave. What may be most shocking to the
modern reader is the king's order in the first place.

The *Targum* translates *d'var hamalkah* (the example of the queen) as "the word of
the queen's command" and hence understands this verse to mean that Vashti actually
ordered the wives of the kingdom to mock their husbands, just as she had when the
king ordered her to appear before him and she did not do so.

אː‏יח וְהַיּוֹם הַזֶּה תֹּאמַרְנָה שָׂרוֹת פָּרַס־וּמָדַי אֲשֶׁר שָׁמְעוּ אֶת־דְּבַר
הַמַּלְכָּה לְכֹל שָׂרֵי הַמֶּלֶךְ וּכְדַי בִּזָּיוֹן וָקָצֶף:

1:18 "TODAY IT WILL BE THE NOBLEWOMEN OF PERSIA AND
MEDIA WHO, HAVING HEARD OF THE EXAMPLE OF THE
QUEEN, WILL SAY THE SAME TO THE KING'S NOBLES—
THERE WILL BE MORE THAN ENOUGH CONTEMPT AND
FRUSTRATION.

The argument being made by the author is that the queen's example will proceed
down the pyramid of social class. Today it will be the wives of nobility. Tomorrow it

will be the wives of a lower order. Vashti's defiance has infected the entire society. We follow Koehler-Baumgartner (p. 1125) in translating *katzef* as "frustration."

The *Targum* reads *d'var hamalkah* (the example of the queen) in the previous verse as "the word of the queen's command" but takes it to mean "obeying the command" in this verse. The noble wives of Persia and Media would take counsel to do to their husbands what Vashti had done to hers. The *Targum* translates the last three words in a plaintive manner: "Who can bear the measure of mocking laughter and anger?"

Rashi sees the verse as a terse statement of the noblewomen telling their husbands about Vashti's defiance (rather than the king's noblemen telling one another). While Rashi translates *k'dai* as "much," we have taken the context into consideration when translating it idiomatically as "more than enough."

Ibn Ezra understands the first two words of the verse, *v'hayom hazeh* (today), as "no sooner than it is spoken, it is acted on" and the last three words as locating "contempt and frustration" between husband and wife.

אִם־עַל־הַמֶּלֶךְ טוֹב יֵצֵא דְבַר־מַלְכוּת מִלְּפָנָיו וְיִכָּתֵב בְּדָתֵי פָרַס־ **א:יט**
וּמָדַי וְלֹא יַעֲבוֹר אֲשֶׁר לֹא־תָבוֹא וַשְׁתִּי לִפְנֵי הַמֶּלֶךְ אֲחַשְׁוֵרוֹשׁ
וּמַלְכוּתָהּ יִתֵּן הַמֶּלֶךְ לִרְעוּתָהּ הַטּוֹבָה מִמֶּנָּה:

1:19 "I F IT PLEASES THE KING, LET A ROYAL PROCLAMATION BE ISSUED. AND LET IT BE SO WRITTEN IN THE LAWS OF PERSIA AND MEDIA THAT IT CANNOT BE ANNULLED SO THAT VASHTI MAY NEVER AGAIN ENTER THE KING'S PRESENCE. LET THE KING BESTOW HER ROYAL STATUS ON ANOTHER WOMAN BETTER THAN SHE.

In its translation, the *Targum* adds that Vashti is to lose more than her royal status— "let the king decree that she lose her head." Rashi assumes that the *Targum*'s translation is correct and explains that the "royal proclamation" is one of vengeance. He also thinks that the proclamation is to be sent out to all wives in order to warn them of the dire consequences of refusing to obey their husbands, pointing out that Vashti was killed because she refused to come before her husband.

א:כ וְנִשְׁמַע פִּתְגָם הַמֶּלֶךְ אֲשֶׁר־יַעֲשֶׂה בְּכָל־מַלְכוּתוֹ כִּי רַבָּה הִיא וְכָל־הַנָּשִׁים יִתְּנוּ יְקָר לְבַעְלֵיהֶן לְמִגָּדוֹל וְעַד־קָטָן:

1:20 "WHEN THE KING'S DECISION THAT HE IS ABOUT TO ACT UPON WILL BE USED [AS LEVERAGE TO CONTROL THE BEHAVIOR OF WOMEN] THROUGHOUT HIS VAST REALM, THEN WILL ALL THE WIVES HONOR THEIR HUSBANDS, FROM THE GREATEST AMONG THEM TO THE LEAST."

It seems that the decision the king is about to make must be quite severe if it is to serve as an example. He thinks that it will make a statement to all of the women in the kingdom—and scare them into obedience.

א:כא וַיִּיטַב הַדָּבָר בְּעֵינֵי הַמֶּלֶךְ וְהַשָּׂרִים וַיַּעַשׂ הַמֶּלֶךְ כִּדְבַר מְמוּכָן:

1:21 THE KING AND THE NOBLES ACCEPTED THE PROPOSAL, AND THE KING DID WHAT MEMUCAN SUGGESTED.

This is a straightforward verse. The king does exactly what is proposed.

א:כב וַיִּשְׁלַח סְפָרִים אֶל־כָּל־מְדִינוֹת הַמֶּלֶךְ אֶל־מְדִינָה וּמְדִינָה כִּכְתָבָהּ וְאֶל־עַם וָעָם כִּלְשׁוֹנוֹ לִהְיוֹת כָּל־אִישׁ שֹׂרֵר בְּבֵיתוֹ וּמְדַבֵּר כִּלְשׁוֹן עַמּוֹ:

1:22 HE SENT DISPATCHES TO ALL THE PROVINCES OF THE KING, TO EACH PROVINCE IN THEIR OWN [ALPHABET] SCRIPT, AND TO EACH PEOPLE IN THEIR OWN LAN-GUAGE SO THAT EVERY MAN COULD RULE IN HIS OWN HOME AND SPEAK IN HIS OWN PEOPLE'S LANGUAGE.

The king so feared the potential fallout of Vashti's actions that he had the royal edict declaring her fate issued in every local language and script used in the kingdom.

To emphasize the importance of this process and of the edict, the *Targum* adds that the dispatches are sealed by the royal signet ring. Since the reader might wonder what exactly is contained in the edict, the *Targum* even imagines the text of the royal dispatch: "O you peoples, nations, and languages who dwell in my kingdom, take care that every man rule over his wife and force her to speak his language and talk to him."

Perhaps following the *Targum*, Rashi interprets "speak in his own people's language" as the husband forcing his wife to learn his language if it is not her native tongue. While the text and Rashi are speaking of a literal difference in language, we might suggest that the verse is speaking to the differences between the ways women and men communicate. Thus, the edict demands that women speak in their husbands' "language," that is, the way men speak.

Ibn Ezra actually reads the last clause to mean that one should not change one's customary language to speak in another language. He notes that some think that this command was enacted just to save the king from shame. Not wanting men to have to change their behaviors to accommodate their wives at all, Ibn Ezra indicates that *shoreir b'veito* (rule in his own home) means "to control his wife."

Darius

Darius was the king of Persia (ca. 549–486/485 B.C.E.) who succeeded Cyrus.

Nebuchadnezzar

Sometimes referred to in the Bible as Nebuchadrezzar, Nebuchadnezzar was king of Babylon and lived from 605 to 562 B.C.E. He captured Jerusalem, destroyed the Temple, and exiled the masses. The period of the exile, 586–538 B.C.E., is known as the Babylonian exile.

Cyrus

Cyrus the Great (ca. 576/590–529 B.C.E.), also called Cyrus the Elder, was Cyrus II of Persia, who founded the Persian Empire (now Iran) under the Achaemenid dynasty. He accomplished this task by joining together two tribes: the Medes and the Persians.

Shishak, King of Egypt

Shishak (sometimes spelled Shishaq), king of Egypt, is best known for his military campaign through the Land of Israel, as noted in various places in the Bible (I Kings 11:40, 14:25; II Chronicles 12:2–9). He provided refuge to Jeroboam during the later years of the reign of Solomon. Upon Solomon's death, Jeroboam became king of the breakaway tribes in the north. This group of tribes became the Kingdom of Israel, also known as the Northern Kingdom. In the fifth year of the reign of Rehoboam (ca. 926–917 B.C.E.), Shishak swept through the Kingdom of Judah with a powerful army in support of his ally. Shishak captured a number of cities of Judah, including Jerusalem, where he pillaged the Temple and carried away the shields of gold that Solomon had made.

Sennacherib

Sennacherib succeeded his father Sargon II on the Assyrian throne, ruling from 705 to 681 B.C.E. His reign was challenged by revolts several times, each of which he successfully defeated. Led by Hezekiah, a rebellion—supported by Egypt—broke out in Judah in 701 B.C.E. As a result, Sennacherib was able to sack many cites in Judah. While he laid siege to Jerusalem, he was unable to pillage the city and soon returned to Nineveh. According to the account of II Kings 19:35, God sent forth an angel that struck down 185,000 Assyrian soldiers.

Hezekiah

Following the death of his father, King Ahaz, Hezekiah ascended the throne in Jerusalem (727–698 B.C.E.), where he made extensive religious and policy reforms. In particular, he renewed worship of the God of Israel, following a long period of time during which idol worship had taken root in Jerusalem. According to II Kings 18:4, "He [Hezekiah] abolished the shrines and smashed the pillars and cut down the sacred post. He also broke into pieces the bronze serpent which Moses had made, for until that time the Israelites had been offering sacrifices to it." Hezekiah also renewed the pilgrimage to Jerusalem for Passover and invited the remnants of the tribe of Israel who had not gone into Assyrian exile to join in the festival celebrations (see II Chronicles 30:13, 30:26).

Isaiah criticized Hezekiah's political approach—he had asked Egypt to help fend off Assyrian expansion (Isaiah 31:1)—since the prophet believed that the Assyrian conquests were a sign to resume the worship of God.

Sanhedrin

The Sanhedrin was the ancient Jewish court system made up of seventy-one judges. While there were smaller religious Sanhedrins in every town in the Land of Israel, during the Temple period the Great Sanhedrin was the supreme religious body. The Sanhedrin system functioned until the abolishment of the Rabbinic patriarchate around 425 C.E.

GLEANINGS

The Book of Esther

To one unfamiliar with the role this book has played in the life of the Jew through the centuries, the high estimate put upon it must seem extravagant indeed. Many a modern scholar, who looks into the synagogue from the outside, could not help but wonder at the extraordinary place this book has won in Jewish tradition. Yet, to the Jew, this Scroll, which is read in the synagogue from year to year on the feast of Purim, is more than a book, even a holy book; it is a record of his tragic fate and a token of his eternity. To him, Haman is not solely a person but a destructive force among men, to be curbed and overcome. Esther and Mordecai are not characters in a romance; they are living figures who war perpetually against hate and cruelty, who forever bring redemption to their people. To the Jew, the Book of Esther, even when it wears the guise of fiction, mirrors most truly the tragedy of his life and the inevitable course of his destiny.

Israel Bettan, *The Five Scrolls*
(Cincinnati: Union of American Hebrew Congregations, 1950), 200–201

Reaching for Joy Every Day

Eventually, we have to take off the masks, to return the archetypes that have come to the surface back to their internal home. But once we have been with them, once we have experienced the infinite joy that comes when we recognize them, we want to be energized like that and to feel that joy as often as we can.

There are two kinds of joy in this world. The first kind is the one we can experience all the time, the kind of joy that says we look happy. We even act as if we are happy, but no one—sometimes not even ourselves—knows if it is real, if it is true joy....

And then there is the other kind of joy, the joy that is at the deepest part of our being, the joy that touches the deepest part of our souls. This is the joy we feel when we are in touch with who and what we really are, with what "makes us or breaks us" as human beings: the joy we feel the moment our child emerges from the womb; the moment our son is called to the Torah as a Bar Mitzvah; the moment we walk our daughter to the *chuppah*. It is a joy we feel that is not dependent on any outside situation or circumstance, any other person or thing. It is the joy we feel when we've done our best and when we've been our best.

Purim teaches us to enjoy this second kind of joy—to get rid of the masks of false joy and to reach for the inner joy that comes when inhibition is gone, when the real self is revealed, when we find and touch the deepest recesses of our being.

Wayne Dosick, *Soul Judaism: Dancing with God into a New Era*
(Woodstock, VT: Jewish Lights Publishing, 1999), 137

The Simplicity of Purim

Purim is deceptively simple. On the surface, Megillat Esther (the Purim scroll) is a charming melodrama: We have Hardhearted Haman, the wicked vizier; simple Addlepated Ahashverosh, the dotty banker/king who "sells the mortgage" to the scheming villain; sweet Excellent Esther, the beauty (and her family), menaced by Haman's advances; Mild-mannered Mordecai, the good hero who finally saves the old homestead. No wonder the atmosphere of synagogue and the community on this day is all fun and games, masquerade and mummers, drinking, partying, and gift-giving.

Yet appearances can be deceptive. Purim, which supports enormous theological freight, may well be the darkest, most depressing holiday of the Jewish calendar. Its laughter is Pagliacci's—a hair's breadth away from despair. While Purim's authenticity as history has been challenged, it is really the holiday that grew out of Jewish history. More than anything else, it is *the* holiday of the Diaspora; it reflects and affirms the experience of the Jewish people living as a minority outside the land of Israel. In its own way, it offers a special guide to Jews who plan to continue living in Diaspora despite the fact that, after two thousand years, the road to Jerusalem is open to any and every Jew who wants to go there.

Irving Greenberg, *The Jewish Way: Living the Holidays*
(New York: Simon & Schuster, 1988), 224

Vashti/Esther: Two Faces of the Same Woman

Megillat Esther has been understood as a fantasy of Jewish power written in a time of Jewish powerlessness. But the megillah actually tells two parallel stories. The primary story is about how Jews in the Diaspora became victims to the whims of power, and then, in the "happy" conclusion, the victors. The secondary story, a story about women and men, follows a similar course, beginning with a wife who is banished when she refuses to obey her husband and concluding with a wife who is listened to and given a significant amount of power. In both stories edicts are issued that threaten the rights of an entire group—Jews and women. Both edicts are eventually subverted through the cunning and courage of Esther and Mordecai. Yet, only one of these subversions is celebrated in our communal observance of Purim.

With the new ritual of waving Esther/Vashti Purim flags, we encourage our communities to celebrate and more deeply explore both of Purim's stories. Purim thus becomes both a celebration of and reflection on Jewish pride and perseverance and an opportunity to honor women's power in the face of those who fear it. . . .

Currently, the rituals and symbols associated with Purim do not evoke either Esther or Vashti. At least symbolically, the fact that the grager and its noise are the prominent symbols and sounds of Purim serve to put Haman, hatred, and sometimes valorization of violent retribution at the center of communal celebrations of Purim. Even though the purpose of the grager is to drown out Haman's name, in actuality it reifies his presence in the sanctuary. . . .

By placing Esther and Vashti on the same flag, we are also challenging ourselves to move beyond the dichotomy of bad queen/good queen (and good feminist/bad feminist) and embrace a wider spectrum of possibility for women's leadership. For much of Jewish interpretive tradition, Vashti was the bad queen and Esther the good one. Then, in the early days of Jewish feminism, Vashti was resurrected and celebrated for her open defiance of the king and her powerful defense of her body and sexuality. Not surprisingly, as Vashti's popularity grew, Esther fell out of favor. Feminists were not sure they could accept two different models of powerful women. For some, Esther suddenly became a negative symbol for all women who use their sexuality, enjoy their beauty, fear confrontation, and remain married to power. These interpretations of Esther minimized her courage in directly confronting Ahasuerus and Haman, and in "coming out" as a Jew after years of hiding her identity. They also ignore Esther's powerful role as an innovator of communal ritual action in her calling for a public fast. . . .

It is time for us to make room in our myths and in our communities for more than one model of leadership. It is time for us to learn from both Esther and Vashti, from both the Jewish women in our texts and the non-Jewish women (and men). It is time to celebrate women's power and to question the ways we have wielded it over others. And, with humor and deep conviction, it is time for us to take the holiday of Purim and, through new ritual, use it to tell our community a new story about who we are, what we value, and what we need to do to build a better world....

Tamara Cohen, "Taking Back Purim," in *A Different Purim Sound:*
Waving Flags and Ringing Bells, An Exhibition of Esther and Vashti Purim Flags
by Jewish Artists (New York: Ma'yan, n.d.)

Purim and Passover

We celebrate Purim one month before Passover. It is, in fact, a bawdy Passover. The destruction of Haman is a bawdy version of the destruction of the Pharaoh. And the victory of Esther is a bawdy version of the victory of the Song of Songs, which we read on Passover. It is a woman who leads the Song of Songs, and some modern readers think the Song celebrates a kind of flowing spirituality that arises from women's experience. Just as Passover according to tradition cannot be fulfilled unless we read the Song of Songs in addition to the Haggadah, so Purim could not be celebrated without Esther alongside Mordechai.

What does it mean that we celebrate a bawdy Purim just one month before the sublimity of Pesach? Why is it that—in exploring the same themes—at Purim we interrupt the Scroll with noisemaking, with laughter, and with getting drunk, while at Passover we interrupt the Haggadah with Four Questions and with four serious cups of wine?

When the original history happened, the sublime liberation of Exodus came long before the farce of Purim. But when we finish living that history and begin to learn it, absorb it into our lives, digest it so that we can make a holy future, then it may be important for us to laugh first, to let the farce come first. For power is funny, and those who hold power are ridiculous. The first stage of liberation is that we learn to laugh at them.

But power is also profound, and liberation is also at the root of all the universe. Having learned to laugh, we become ready to seek our freedom seriously. There is a time to laugh—and then there is a time to ask questions.

Arthur Waskow, *Seasons of Our Joy: A Handbook of Jewish Festivals*
(New York: Bantam Books, 1982), 126–27

CHAPTER TWO

ב:א אַחַר הַדְּבָרִים הָאֵלֶּה כְּשֹׁךְ חֲמַת הַמֶּלֶךְ אֲחַשְׁוֵרוֹשׁ זָכַר אֶת־
וַשְׁתִּי וְאֵת אֲשֶׁר־עָשָׂתָה וְאֵת אֲשֶׁר־נִגְזַר עָלֶיהָ:

2:1 AFTER ALL OF THIS, WHEN KING AHASUERUS CALMED
DOWN, HE REMEMBERED VASHTI, WHAT SHE HAD DONE,
AND WHAT HAD BEEN DONE TO HER.

Perhaps the text should read, "When he sobered up...." The author is suggesting that Ahasuerus regrets what he has done and is particularly unsettled by the far-reaching impact of the edict that he allowed his advisors to convince him to issue.

In its translation, the *Targum* chooses to tell the story a little differently. While it wants to furnish details that might be missing from the verse, the *Targum* also does not want to minimize the power of the king, especially since it will be pivotal later in the narrative. The *Targum* describes Ahasuerus as the witless victim of scheming advisors: "When the king became sober, his nobles said to him, 'You are the one who condemned her to death for what she did.' He answered, 'I never ordered her execution. All I ordered was that she not come into my presence again and that she lose her royal status.'... They said to him, 'That's not so. On the advice of seven nobles, you did order her execution.' Erupting in anger, the king ordered those seven nobles to be hanged."

The text doesn't say what it is that Ahasuerus actually remembers. For Rashi, it is Vashti's beauty that the king "remembered." The loss of that beauty saddens him.

ב:ב וַיֹּאמְרוּ נַעֲרֵי־הַמֶּלֶךְ מְשָׁרְתָיו יְבַקְשׁוּ לַמֶּלֶךְ נְעָרוֹת בְּתוּלוֹת
טוֹבוֹת מַרְאֶה:

2:2 THEN THE YOUNG SERVANTS OF THE KING SAID, "LET
YOUNG BEAUTIFUL VIRGINS BE FOUND FOR THE KING.

The king's servants realize that they are vulnerable. One could never tell what the
king would do in the midst of his remorse. So they suggest something that might
appease him and perhaps make up for the loss of Vashti. It is challenging to translate
this verse idiomatically. There is a tendency to want to translate the verse in an active
voice and change the verb *y'vakshu* (let there be sought) to "find," that is, "Let's find
young beautiful virgins." We leave it in the passive voice as "Let young virgins be
found for the king," which leaves the actors ambiguous. The emphasis of "virgins"
reflects the position of women in the ancient world as sexual objects. Those who
controlled the society wanted to be the first to use such objects.

ב:ג וְיַפְקֵד הַמֶּלֶךְ פְּקִידִים בְּכָל־מְדִינוֹת מַלְכוּתוֹ וְיִקְבְּצוּ אֶת־כָּל־
נַעֲרָה־בְתוּלָה טוֹבַת מַרְאֶה אֶל־שׁוּשַׁן הַבִּירָה אֶל־בֵּית הַנָּשִׁים
אֶל־יַד הֵגֶא סְרִיס הַמֶּלֶךְ שֹׁמֵר הַנָּשִׁים וְנָתוֹן תַּמְרֻקֵיהֶן:

2:3 "LET THE KING APPOINT OFFICERS THROUGHOUT THE
PROVINCES OF HIS KINGDOM. LET THEM COLLECT EVERY
BEAUTIFUL YOUNG VIRGIN. LET THEM BE BROUGHT TO
THE FORTRESS OF SHUSHAN. LET THEM BE PLACED IN
THE HOUSE OF WOMEN. LET THEM BE SET UNDER
CONTROL OF HEGE, THE KING'S EUNUCH WHO IS IN
CHARGE OF WOMEN, AND LET COSMETICS BE BROUGHT
FOR THEM.

The structure of the verse lays out a step-by-step process that the king's officers should
follow if the king accepts the recommendation of his servants. Whatever one's
opinion of beauty contests, it seems that this is what is being described. This is perhaps the reason why Purim pageants are held for young girls as part of the celebration

of Purim. But there is much more to this verse. It implies that the women should be brought to the king, regardless of their own desire. As implied by the previous verse, when they get there, they will become part of the king's harem, to be used for his sexual pleasure. Since the king lives in the midst of a fortress, the implication is that these women will be unable to escape, and that no one will be able to rescue them. Once they are in the fortress, they will remain there.

In order to emphasize the objectification of women that is clearly present in this verse, we choose to translate *v'yikb'tzu* (gather, assemble) as "collect." People may "gather" or "assemble" on their own, but objects are "collected" by someone else. The young women in this story are not asked if they would like to join the king; they are ordered to do so.

The *Targum* uses the Greek loan word *apitropin* (guardians, administrators) to describe these *p'kidim* (officers). In its translation, the *Targum* emphasizes that there is a bathhouse in the "house of women," indicating that there is a reason for women to want to come to the palace. A bathhouse was a luxury in the ancient world that most could not afford to enjoy regularly. Rashi thinks that the officers whom the king assigns to this task are chosen because they can identify the beautiful women in the region. He explains that the "cosmetics" (*tamrukeihen*) contain various ingredients to clarify, purify, and soften the skin. This might act as a further enticement for the women, and it also emphasizes the king's interest in their physical beauty.

ב:ד וְהַנַּעֲרָה אֲשֶׁר תִּיטַב בְּעֵינֵי הַמֶּלֶךְ תִּמְלֹךְ תַּחַת וַשְׁתִּי וַיִּיטַב הַדָּבָר בְּעֵינֵי הַמֶּלֶךְ וַיַּעַשׂ כֵּן:

2:4 "Let the young woman who pleases the king reign in place of Vashti." The idea pleased the king, and this he did.

It seems that the servants' suggestion speaks to the king's desires, and so he accepts it. This pattern of behavior—accepting the advice of others—will prove to be important later in the story as the king accepts the suggestion of Haman.

ב:ה אִישׁ יְהוּדִי הָיָה בְּשׁוּשַׁן הַבִּירָה וּשְׁמוֹ מָרְדֳּכַי בֶּן יָאִיר בֶּן־שִׁמְעִי
בֶּן־קִישׁ אִישׁ יְמִינִי:

2:5 There was a Jew living in the fortress of Shushan
of the tribe of Benjamin named Mordecai son of
Yair, son of Shimei, son of Kish.

This verse introduces us to Mordecai. By identifying where he lives, the author lets
readers know that he is a man of prominence. Otherwise, he would not be enjoying
the benefits of living in a protected area. The *Targum* wants to make sure that we
know about Mordecai's identity, since this will prove to be important later in the story.
The *Targum* also explains Mordecai's family history so that readers will see his connection to the other events in the Bible and to Esther. It adds that Mordecai is ''a pious
man who prayed to God for his people. . . . He was named Mordecai, because he was
compared to *meira dachya* (pure myrrh). He was called son of Yair and son of Shimei;
[however] Shimei son of Gera was the one who cursed David [II Samuel 16:5–13].
[At a later date], Joab [in our text of Samuel, it is Abishai] wished to kill him [Shimei]
[II Samuel 19:21–22]. David would not permit Shimei's execution because through
the spirit of prophecy he foresaw that from him would proceed Mordecai and Esther.
When Shimei could no longer procreate, David commanded his son Solomon to kill
him [I Kings 2:8–9].''

Rashi is not satisfied with the *Targum*'s explanation and suggests that the word
Y'hudi (Jew) refers to those who went into exile with the kings of Judah. Even if they
were from another tribe, they were called *Y'hudim*, ''Jews.'' He takes *y'mini* to mean
''from the tribe of Benjamin'' and alludes to the Rabbinic wordplay on *y'mini*
(''distinguished in behavior,'' in Babylonian Talmud, *M'gillah* 12b). Ibn Ezra adds that
ben Kish indicates some connection to Saul (I Samuel 9:1 and Babylonian Talmud,
M'gillah 13b). However, he cautions readers, were this Kish the father of King Saul, it
would have been noted in the text.

ב:ו אֲשֶׁר הָגְלָה מִירוּשָׁלַיִם עִם־הַגֹּלָה אֲשֶׁר הָגְלְתָה עִם יְכָנְיָה מֶלֶךְ־
יְהוּדָה אֲשֶׁר הֶגְלָה נְבוּכַדְנֶצַּר מֶלֶךְ בָּבֶל:

2:6 He [Mordecai] had been exiled from Jerusalem by
Nebuchadnezzar, king of Babylon, in the same
group that had been exiled with Jehoiachin, king
of Judah.

This verse is a reference to what is described in II Kings 24:12ff. But there appear to
be two spellings of the Hebrew name of the king of Judah. In Kings, it is given as
Y'hoyachin. It is spelled as *Y'chonyah* in the Book of Esther.

In its expansion of the verse, the *Targum* explains how Mordecai got to Shushan.
This question emerges directly from the text. If Mordecai was sent into exile to
Babylon, how did he end up in Shushan? And how did Esther, as well? The *Targum*
tells us that "when Cyrus and Darius conquered Babylon, Mordecai—together with
Daniel and all of the Israelites—left Babylon and went with Cyrus to dwell in the
fortress of Shushan."

ב:ז וַיְהִי אֹמֵן אֶת־הֲדַסָּה הִיא אֶסְתֵּר בַּת־דֹּדוֹ כִּי אֵין לָהּ אָב וָאֵם
וְהַנַּעֲרָה יְפַת־תֹּאַר וְטוֹבַת מַרְאֶה וּבְמוֹת אָבִיהָ וְאִמָּהּ לְקָחָהּ
מָרְדֳּכַי לוֹ לְבַת:

2:7 Because she [Esther] had neither father nor
mother, Mordecai took care of his cousin
Hadassah, known as Esther. When her father
and mother died, he had adopted her as his own
daughter. Now the young woman was extremely
beautiful in face and in form.

This verse explains to the reader the relationship between Esther and Mordecai, but
we still know very little about either character. For example, we don't know how
Esther's parents died or when she was adopted. And did Mordecai have a spouse or
children of his own? Nor do we know why Esther has two names. Since the verse is

difficult to translate, we attempt to make it clear to the English reader by changing the word order to fit our translation.

Although same commentators have understood Esther to be Mordecai's niece, the text is clear about their relationship. Esther was the daughter of Abihail (see Esther 2:15), who was Mordecai's uncle. That makes Mordecai and Esther cousins. Mordecai adopted Esther after his uncle's death. Some probably assume that they were uncle and niece because of the difference in their ages. It is logical to assume that an orphaned infant raised as one's own child is of a younger generation and not of the same generation.

Much has been made of the two names of Mordecai's adopted daughter. According to Koehler-Bamgartner, Esther is derived from the Babylonian *Istar*, the goddess of love, fertility, and war (p. 76), and Hadassah is derived from the Akkadian, in which it means "bride just married" (p. 239). Hadassah may also be the feminine form of the Hebrew *hadas* (myrtle). The combination of meanings can be seen as an attempt to characterize the story's heroine as an "everywoman."

The *Targum*, like the Talmud (Babylonian Talmud, *M'gillah* 13a), is able to explain both names and offer insight into the character of the young woman who is the hero of the entire story. Because the Aramaic for "myrtle" (*asa*) has a homonym meaning healer or physician, we learn that Myrtle/Esther was so called because of her righteousness, as the righteous are compared to the healers of the world. Because the last three letters of the name Esther in Hebrew (*samech, tav, reish*) spell the word *seiter* (secret), we learn that the young woman was given this name because she displayed such extreme modesty in her home that she had never seen the face of a man other than Mordecai (whom the *Targum* tells us is seventy-five years old), who adopted and raised her. Such an explanation of modesty emerges from an extremely narrow reading of Jewish tradition. Answering the question that perplexes any reader of the story, the *Targum* tells us that Esther's father died while Esther's mother was pregnant with her and then her mother died during childbirth.

Rashi tries to help us understand the relationship between Mordecai and Esther by quoting a text from the same section of the Talmud noted above. He reads *l'vat*, "for a daughter," as *l'vayit*, "for a household," that is, "as his wife." This implies that Mordecai actually married Esther (see Babylonian Talmud, *M'gillah* 13a).

Ibn Ezra is not satisfied with either of these explanations and shares with his readers the surprising view of Y'hoshua ben Karcha from the same page of the Talmud used by both aforementioned commentators. Ibn Ezra tells us that Esther had the name Myrtle because her complexion was a pale green, as the color of the shrub. (Rashi, in a comment on the Talmud passage quoted by Ibn Ezra—but not used by Rashi in his commentary on Esther—claims that it was an act of God that made Esther appear beautiful to Ahasuerus and others, since her face had a green cast to it.) While Ibn Ezra is not convinced that Mordecai actually took Esther as his wife, he does not dismiss it as a possibility and suggests that perhaps Mordecai was merely desirous of doing so. If either position is the case, it casts a less than benign light on a man whom tradition usually colors as Esther's benefactor and protector, as well as a righteous individual.

ב:ח וַיְהִי בְּהִשָּׁמַע דְּבַר־הַמֶּלֶךְ וְדָתוֹ וּבְהִקָּבֵץ נְעָרוֹת רַבּוֹת אֶל־שׁוּשַׁן הַבִּירָה אֶל־יַד הֵגַי וַתִּלָּקַח אֶסְתֵּר אֶל־בֵּית הַמֶּלֶךְ אֶל־יַד הֵגַי שֹׁמֵר הַנָּשִׁים:

2:8 MANY YOUNG WOMEN WERE GATHERED INTO THE FORTRESS OF SHUSHAN UNDER THE CONTROL OF HEGAI, FOLLOWING THE ANNOUNCEMENT OF THE KING'S ORDER AND EDICT. ESTHER ALSO WAS TAKEN INTO THE KING'S PALACE UNDER THE CONTROL OF HEGAI, THE WOMEN'S GUARD.

This verse tells us that the competition for the role of queen is extensive. It isn't clear how many of these women come voluntarily or if they are required to respond to the king's request, since it is issued as a royal edict or decree. The *Targum* wants us to understand that Esther does not come willingly. To stress its position, the *Targum* translates "taken" as "led away by force."

ב:ט וַתִּיטַב הַנַּעֲרָה בְעֵינָיו וַתִּשָּׂא חֶסֶד לְפָנָיו וַיְבַהֵל אֶת־תַּמְרוּקֶיהָ
וְאֶת־מָנוֹתֶהָ לָתֵת לָהּ וְאֵת שֶׁבַע הַנְּעָרוֹת הָרְאֻיוֹת לָתֶת־לָהּ
מִבֵּית הַמֶּלֶךְ וַיְשַׁנֶּהָ וְאֶת־נַעֲרוֹתֶיהָ לְטוֹב בֵּית הַנָּשִׁים:

2:9 The young woman [Esther] pleased him [Ahasuerus]. She so won his favor that he immediately gave her special ointments and foods. He also assigned her seven young women (as servants) from the king's palace, transferring her and them to the best place in the king's palace.

This verse presents the translator with some difficulties. According to Koehler-Baumgartner (p. 1758), *tamrukeha/tamruk* has a number of related meanings: "an aid to beauty," "oil of anointing," or "a woman's cosmetic preparation." We choose to translate the word as "special ointments." *Manoteha/maneh* means "share," "portion," or "obligatory supplies" according to Koehler-Baumgartner (p. 1598). We translate this word as "special foods." While we follow Koehler-Baumgartner (p. 1598) in translating *vay'shaneha* as "transferred," we adjust the reading in English to "transferring."

It is clear from this verse that Ahasuerus is immediately smitten with Esther's beauty. While he can simply order her to participate in his harem, he attempts to win her over with gifts. Additionally, he assigns a staff from his own retinue to care for her. Their responsibility, however, will be to make sure she retains her physical beauty for him. In keeping with what we know about kings and their harems, these servants may even be responsible for instructing Esther sexually in preparation for entering the king's bed.

While Rashi does not mention Hegai in the verse in which he appears for the first time (2:8), he does so here. He explains that Hegai acts quickly to give preferential treatment to Esther, as the king is clearly taken by Esther's beauty. Rashi also tells his readers that each young woman who participates in the so-called beauty contest is assigned seven female servants. This is an allusion to the discussion in the Talmud between Rav and Shmuel (Babylonian Talmud, *M'gillah* 13a) about the meaning of "seven" in this verse as an indicator of either the days of the week or the variety of foods. Although Rashi offers no explanation of his own, he rejects both explanations. The former seems to us to be the more plausible explanation; regardless, the number "seven" is important anytime it is used in Jewish sacred literature, for it refers to the seven days of creation.

For Ibn Ezra, *vay'shaneha* (transferred or changed) refers to the food served rather than a reference to the place in the harem in which Esther and her maidservants are placed. If they are given the "best place" in the king's palace, as the author tells us in this verse, then the king surely means Esther to be the primary woman in his harem, namely, his queen. Alternatively, if the food is changed, this means that the king provides for her abundantly.

בּ:יי לֹא־הִגִּידָה אֶסְתֵּר אֶת־עַמָּהּ וְאֶת־מוֹלַדְתָּהּ כִּי מָרְדֳּכַי צִוָּה עָלֶיהָ
אֲשֶׁר לֹא־תַגִּיד:

2:10 BECAUSE MORDECAI TOLD HER NOT TO DO SO, ESTHER DID NOT TELL [THE KING] ABOUT HER PEOPLE OR HER FAMILY.

By this point in the story, readers may wonder about the extent to which Esther discloses details about her family life. On the one hand, one would think that the king would be interested in knowing a great deal about the woman he chooses as queen. On the other hand, he may have little interest in knowing anything about her and may only be interested in taking her into his harem and into his bed.

Readers also may be puzzled as to why Mordecai instructs Esther to keep her identity secret. It is unusual that a sacred text would imply that it is not appropriate for a hero of the Jewish people to proudly express her Jewish identity. The *Targum* explains that Mordecai thought to himself that since Vashti had been executed merely because she did not obey the king's command to display her beauty before his courtiers, if Esther now revealed her lineage, the king might get angry and kill her and destroy her people.

Rashi offers an alternative explanation for Mordecai's advice. Mordecai hoped that if Esther did not disclose her background, the people in the palace would think that she came from a lowly background and the king would eventually release her. But if she told them that she came from the line of King Saul, they would hold onto her.

Ibn Ezra is not satisfied with either explanation. First he explains the teachings of others. He tells readers that some say that Mordecai makes a mistake by thinking that Ahasuerus would not marry Esther if he knew that she came from the exile. Others claim that the king knew through either a dream or an act of prophecy that Esther would bring salvation to Israel. In Ibn Ezra's opinion, Mordecai acts so that Esther could secretly observe the Torah, specifically by avoiding forbidden food and keeping the Sabbath. He reminds the reader that Esther is, after all, taken against her will into the palace. So much for the notion of a voluntary beauty contest! Had the king realized that Esther was Jewish, he might have forced her to desecrate the Torah or be killed if she refused to do so.

But for Ibn Ezra, this is not enough of an explanation concerning Mordecai's actions. He claims that Mordecai was one of the important leaders of Israel. Mordecai was third in rank of those who came up [to the Land of Israel] with Zerubbabel. However, when he saw that the Temple had not been rebuilt, Mordecai went to Elam, where he achieved high status as a member of the king's court. When Daniel had served in the royal Babylonian court, he had appointed friends to positions of authority. While it not clear how Mordecai gained his status, had he not been one of the king's courtiers prior to the events concerning Esther, the other courtiers would not have allowed him to walk back and forth in front of the courtyard of the royal harem, as noted in the next verse.

ב:יא וּבְכָל־יוֹם וָיוֹם מָרְדֳּכַי מִתְהַלֵּךְ לִפְנֵי חֲצַר בֵּית־הַנָּשִׁים לָדַעַת אֶת־שְׁלוֹם אֶסְתֵּר וּמַה־יֵּעָשֶׂה בָּהּ:

2:11 MORDECAI WOULD WALK BACK AND FORTH IN THE COURTYARD OF THE HAREM DAILY TO FIND OUT HOW ESTHER WAS AND WHAT WAS HAPPENING TO HER.

We can anticipate this verse from Ibn Ezra's comment on the previous verse. The author uses this verse to show readers the ease with which Mordecai makes his way through the palace area, especially near the king's harem, where such freedoms are severely limited. Thus, it is clear that Mordecai had the status of a nobleman. The *Targum* adds the word *m'tzalei* (would pray) to show that Mordecai takes these walks in order to pray.

Rashi uses the opportunity of this verse—and Mordecai's constant concern for Esther's well-being—to indicate that Mordecai is one of only two righteous persons to whom a sign of future redemption is given. (David is the only other person privileged in such a way.) Mordecai thinks that the only reason that a woman as righteous as Esther would go to Ahasuerus's bed—willingly or not—is that in doing so she would be able to save the Jewish people.

Since Ibn Ezra takes the word *shalom* as "welfare" (which we have translated as "how [she] was"), he suggests that Mordecai is concerned that Esther might need medical help.

ב:יב וּבְהַגִּיעַ תֹּר נַעֲרָה וְנַעֲרָה לָבוֹא אֶל־הַמֶּלֶךְ אֲחַשְׁוֵרוֹשׁ מִקֵּץ הֱיוֹת
לָהּ כְּדָת הַנָּשִׁים שְׁנֵים עָשָׂר חֹדֶשׁ כִּי כֵּן יִמְלְאוּ יְמֵי מְרוּקֵיהֶן
שִׁשָּׁה חֳדָשִׁים בְּשֶׁמֶן הַמֹּר וְשִׁשָּׁה חֳדָשִׁים בַּבְּשָׂמִים וּבְתַמְרוּקֵי
הַנָּשִׁים:

2:12 THERE WAS A REQUIRED TWELVE-MONTH COSMETIC TREATMENT CONSISTING OF SIX MONTHS' USE OF OIL AND MYRRH AND SIX MONTHS' USE OF PERFUMES AND SPECIAL OINTMENTS DESIGNED FOR WOMEN BEFORE ANY YOUNG WOMAN WOULD HAVE HER TURN TO COME BEFORE KING AHASUERUS.

How does one prepare to go from a "beauty contest" to a king's harem? What goes on behind the closed door of the palace? And what will Esther spend her time doing when she is not in the king's bedroom?

We follow Koehler-Baumgartner (p. 634) in our translation of *markum* (a form from *m'rukeihen* that grammarians call "uninflected") as "cosmetic treatment." Nevertheless, the reader will wonder why it takes so long to prepare to be a royal concubine. Perhaps the treatment is to suggest one of the "perks" of being a king: sex with a young woman so perfumed that he cannot distinguish her from any other woman by smell. Thus, such a concubine would be indistinguishable from any other concubine in terms of her use by the king. A cosmetic treatment of twelve months' duration—with forced compliance—symbolizes the process of objectifying the woman.

For the reader who wants to further understand the treatment, the *Targum* describes the effect of the oil of myrrh: it makes the hair lustrous and improves the skin.

בּ:יג וּבָזֶה הַנַּעֲרָה בָּאָה אֶל־הַמֶּלֶךְ אֵת כָּל־אֲשֶׁר תֹּאמַר יִנָּתֵן לָהּ
לָבוֹא עִמָּהּ מִבֵּית הַנָּשִׁים עַד־בֵּית הַמֶּלֶךְ:

2:13 WHEN THE YOUNG WOMAN WOULD FINALLY GO TO THE KING, SHE WOULD BE GIVEN WHATEVER SHE ASKED FOR TO TAKE ALONG AS SHE MOVED FROM THE HAREM TO THE PALACE.

Reflecting the previous verse, the *Targum* adds the words "after the twelve months" after "finally" to ensure that the reader understands the importance of the sequence of the verse. The *Targum* also tells us that the woman's requests are directed to "officials and officers" of the palace. In a comment not intended to be funny, Rashi suggests that the requests are for musical instruments—undoubtedly to seduce the king—though this conjures up an image of a ragtag band. In an empathetic comment, Ibn Ezra tells us that the young woman receives what she requests to distract her and keep her from becoming depressed. It is clear that some commentators tried to understand Esther's situation and mental state, even if it is glossed over by many others, then and now.

ב:יד בָּעֶרֶב הִיא בָאָה וּבַבֹּקֶר הִיא שָׁבָה אֶל־בֵּית הַנָּשִׁים שֵׁנִי אֶל־יַד
שַׁעֲשְׁגַז סְרִיס הַמֶּלֶךְ שֹׁמֵר הַפִּילַגְשִׁים לֹא־תָבוֹא עוֹד אֶל־הַמֶּלֶךְ
כִּי אִם־חָפֵץ בָּהּ הַמֶּלֶךְ וְנִקְרְאָה בְשֵׁם:

2:14 IN THE EVENING SHE WOULD ARRIVE, AND IN THE
MORNING SHE WOULD LEAVE TO GO TO ANOTHER
HAREM, CONTROLLED BY SHAASHGAZ, THE ROYAL
EUNUCH IN CHARGE OF THE CONCUBINES. ONLY IF
THE KING DESIRED HER AND SUMMONED HER BY NAME
WOULD SHE GO AGAIN TO THE KING.

One can see from this verse that life for Esther and the other royal concubines was
rather bleak: After one night with the king, a concubine is sent on to another harem,
where she remains until the king chooses to summon her again. The *Targum* tries to
render the verse more acceptable by suggesting that the young woman arrives in the
evening "to serve the king" without specifying the service involved. It also changes
the word for concubine to *matronitai* (matrons or ladies).

Ibn Ezra explains that Esther was a virgin before she entered the king's harem. After
she engages with the king sexually, no other man can have sexual relations with her;
such an act would be lese majesty (an offense against the dignity of the sovereign).

ב:טו וּבְהַגִּיעַ תֹּר־אֶסְתֵּר בַּת־אֲבִיחַיִל דֹּד מָרְדֳּכַי אֲשֶׁר לָקַח־לוֹ לְבַת
לָבוֹא אֶל־הַמֶּלֶךְ לֹא בִקְשָׁה דָּבָר כִּי אִם אֶת־אֲשֶׁר יֹאמַר הֵגַי
סְרִיס־הַמֶּלֶךְ שֹׁמֵר הַנָּשִׁים וַתְּהִי אֶסְתֵּר נֹשֵׂאת חֵן בְּעֵינֵי כָּל־
רֹאֶיהָ:

2:15 WHEN IT WAS ESTHER'S TURN—SHE WHO WAS ADOPTED
BY MORDECAI, THE DAUGHTER OF ABIHAIL, HIS UNCLE—
SHE ASKED ONLY FOR WHAT HEGAI, THE ROYAL EUNUCH
IN CHARGE OF THE WOMEN, ADVISED. ESTHER FOUND
FAVOR IN THE EYES OF EVERYONE WHO SAW HER.

Apparently, Esther is so attractive that she captivates anyone who sees her. Anyone—
especially men—would be willing to do anything she asks. While the verse focuses on

Esther's physical beauty, she seems to be charismatic as well, so much so that Hegai is prepared to offer his advice to her. If he were to do something on his own or contrary to what the king asked, he would be risking his life.

בּ:טז וַתִּלָּקַח אֶסְתֵּר אֶל־הַמֶּלֶךְ אֲחַשְׁוֵרוֹשׁ אֶל־בֵּית מַלְכוּתוֹ בַּחֹדֶשׁ
הָעֲשִׂירִי הוּא־חֹדֶשׁ טֵבֵת בִּשְׁנַת־שֶׁבַע לְמַלְכוּתוֹ:

2:16 ESTHER WAS TAKEN TO KING AHASUERUS, INTO THE
ROYAL PALACE, IN THE TENTH MONTH, THE MONTH OF
TEVET, IN THE SEVENTH YEAR OF HIS [AHASUERUS'S]
REIGN.

This verse helps the reader get a sense of timing of the events that take place in the narrative. It reads, however, like an official court document, which is probably what the writer is attempting to parallel. The Targum adds the word *etitah*, "wife," to its translation, understanding Esther's being "taken" as marriage. It also adds the word *idron* (bedroom) so that there would be no doubt as to where Esther is taken.

Although in the ancient world dates were regularly indicated in reference to the year of the king's reign, Rashi tells us that "the tenth month" is mentioned because it is the cool part of the year. He tells us that God decided that would be the time of year that Esther would be brought to the palace—presumably because women looked their best during that time—so that the king would be enthralled by her. Ibn Ezra disagrees. He claims that Tevet is the Aramaic term for the month, originally noted by its Hebrew number.

ב:יז וַיֶּאֱהַב הַמֶּלֶךְ אֶת־אֶסְתֵּר מִכָּל־הַנָּשִׁים וַתִּשָּׂא־חֵן וָחֶסֶד לְפָנָיו מִכָּל־הַבְּתוּלוֹת וַיָּשֶׂם כֶּתֶר־מַלְכוּת בְּרֹאשָׁהּ וַיַּמְלִיכֶהָ תַּחַת וַשְׁתִּי:

2:17 THE KING FELL IN LOVE WITH ESTHER, MORE THAN ANY OTHER WOMAN. MORE THAN ANY OTHER VIRGIN, SHE WON HIS FAVOR AND HIS DEVOTION. HE THEN PUT THE ROYAL CROWN ON HER HEAD AND DECLARED HER TO BE QUEEN IN PLACE OF VASHTI.

Love at first sight—so it seems. Yet, the juxtaposition of previous verses with this verse suggests that the king's ''love'' is much more physical than the love described here. Even so, this verse clearly indicates that Esther wins Ahasuerus's heart and the queen's crown.

In an otherwise literal translation, the *Targum* provides the reader with additional information: ''Ahasuerus removed the *ikonin* (picture or statue) of Vashti from his bedroom and replaced it with one of Esther. He also placed Esther on a second throne where Vashti once sat.''

ב:יח וַיַּעַשׂ הַמֶּלֶךְ מִשְׁתֶּה גָדוֹל לְכָל־שָׂרָיו וַעֲבָדָיו אֵת מִשְׁתֵּה אֶסְתֵּר וַהֲנָחָה לַמְּדִינוֹת עָשָׂה וַיִּתֵּן מַשְׂאֵת כְּיַד הַמֶּלֶךְ:

2:18 THE KING MADE A GREAT BANQUET FOR ALL OF HIS MINISTERS AND OFFICIALS, A BANQUET IN HONOR OF ESTHER. HE PROCLAIMED THE REMISSION OF TAXES FOR ALL THE PROVINCES AND ROYALLY DISTRIBUTED GIFTS.

This is the wedding feast. The king demonstrates his delight with Esther by displaying largess to his subjects. We follow Koehler-Baumgartner (p. 252) in translating *hanachah* as ''the release of taxes,'' although we render it idiomatically with the word ''remission.'' Rashi argues that by sending gifts, Ahasuerus is trying to persuade Esther to reveal her background.

בּ:יט וּבְהִקָּבֵץ בְּתוּלוֹת שֵׁנִית וּמָרְדֳּכַי יֹשֵׁב בְּשַׁעַר-הַמֶּלֶךְ:

2:19 MORDECAI WAS SITTING AT THE PALACE GATE WHEN THE VIRGINS WERE ASSEMBLED A SECOND TIME.

This verse seems to be out of place and would be more fitting between verses 20 and 21. But the reader is still left with the question as to why the young women would be assembled a second time and what the relationship is between where Mordecai is sitting and the assembling of the women. Ibn Ezra suggests that it is Mordecai who has come to the palace gate (literally, "king's gate") a second time. The king's gate or palace gate (as we translate it) seems to be equivalent to the "royal court." Mordecai has previously been there, at the ill-fated banquet for Vashti. Ibn Ezra then goes on to quote a rather disturbing text from the Talmud (Babylonian Talmud, *M'gillah* 13b) that suggests that because the Jews ate at the king's table and drank his wine (that is, nonkosher food and wine), they were condemned to death. If this were the case, then the aspects of the story concerning how Haman came to dislike the Jews and arrange for their death become irrelevant. Instead, Haman is merely a pawn in God's plan to punish the Jewish people.

בּ:כ אֵין אֶסְתֵּר מַגֶּדֶת מוֹלַדְתָּהּ וְאֶת-עַמָּהּ כַּאֲשֶׁר צִוָּה עָלֶיהָ מָרְדֳּכָי
וְאֶת-מַאֲמַר מָרְדֳּכַי אֶסְתֵּר עֹשָׂה כַּאֲשֶׁר הָיְתָה בְאָמְנָה אִתּוֹ:

2:20 AS SHE HAD DONE WHEN MORDECAI BROUGHT HER UP, ESTHER OBEYED HIS BIDDING AND THEREFORE DID NOT REVEAL [TO AHASUERUS ANYTHING ABOUT] HER FAMILY OR PEOPLE.

This verse shows the reader once again that Mordecai does not want Esther to reveal her Jewish background, and she obediently follows his direction, as she has done her entire life. Although we follow Koehler-Baumgartner (p. 65), which translates *omnah* as "guardianship," we elect to translate the term idiomatically as "brought her up."

ב:כא בַּיָּמִים הָהֵם וּמָרְדֳּכַי יוֹשֵׁב בְּשַׁעַר־הַמֶּלֶךְ קָצַף בִּגְתָן וָתֶרֶשׁ שְׁנֵי־
סָרִיסֵי הַמֶּלֶךְ מִשֹּׁמְרֵי הַסַּף וַיְבַקְשׁוּ לִשְׁלֹחַ יָד בַּמֶּלֶךְ אֲחַשְׁוֵרֹשׁ:

2:21 At the time that Mordecai was sitting at the palace gate, two of the doorkeepers, the royal eunuchs Bigthan and Teresh, became so angry that they planned to murder King Ahasuerus.

Any reader would want to know how it is that Mordecai is able to overhear a plot to kill the king. As a privileged person, Mordecai is able to sit at the palace gate, an area where the nobles of the city spend their leisure time. The verse begins with the familiar *bayamim haheim* (in those days), which functions similarly to "once upon a time" in tales and legends. We choose to translate it as "at the time." We also follow Koehler-Baumgartner (p. 763) in translating *shomrei hasaf* as "doorkeepers."

The *Targum* imagines a Rabbinic structure that has Mordecai "in the Sanhedrin that Esther had established in the king's gate." It also provides the reason for both Bigthan and Teresh's anger and their desire to kill the king, something that is not explicated by the author. According to the *Targum*, they are afraid that Esther will install Mordecai in their place. As a result, they plan to kill Esther by means of poison and Ahasuerus with a sword.

Ibn Ezra tells us more about the role of the doorkeepers. He suggests that they guard the innermost portal of the palace. The text doesn't explicitly describe how Mordecai hears about Bigthan and Teresh's plans, but it implies that he simply overhears them. Ibn Ezra suggests that since Mordecai was a member of the Sanhedrin, he knew seventy languages (a metaphor for all of the languages of the world) and thus was able to understand what he overheard. While one might assume that he draws this conclusion from the phrase *Mordecai bilshan* (see Ezra 2:2 and Nehemiah 7:7), since in late biblical Hebrew *balshan* means "linguist" or "translator," Ibn Ezra actually rejects this derivation. Although he agrees with the conclusion, he contends that the term *bilshan* designates a particular person and is not a general term.

ב:כב וַיִּוָּדַע הַדָּבָר לְמָרְדֳּכַי וַיַּגֵּד לְאֶסְתֵּר הַמַּלְכָּה וַתֹּאמֶר אֶסְתֵּר לַמֶּלֶךְ
בְּשֵׁם מָרְדֳּכָי:

2:22 MORDECAI FOUND OUT ABOUT IT AND TOLD QUEEN
ESTHER. IN MORDECAI'S NAME, ESTHER THEN TOLD
THE KING.

While the previous verse only implies that Mordecai finds out about the plot to kill the
king, this verse states it explicitly—although it too does not tell the reader how
Mordecai comes upon this information. The *Targum* translates ''in Mordecai's name''
as *itk'tiv al shum*, ''it was written down in the name of,'' Mordecai. This is the
Targum's way of telling readers that it became part of the permanent record of the
kingdom. This record will play an important role in chapter six, as the story unfolds.
Rashi reminds us that the eunuchs were speaking in their native language, thinking
that no one could understand what they were saying. As the *Targum* mentioned in the
previous verse, Mordecai was an adept linguist and so was able to understand what
they were saying.

ב:כג וַיְבֻקַּשׁ הַדָּבָר וַיִּמָּצֵא וַיִּתָּלוּ שְׁנֵיהֶם עַל־עֵץ וַיִּכָּתֵב בְּסֵפֶר דִּבְרֵי
הַיָּמִים לִפְנֵי הַמֶּלֶךְ:

2:23 WHEN THE MATTER WAS INVESTIGATED, IT WAS FOUND
TO BE TRUE. SO THE TWO WERE HANGED ON THE GAL-
LOWS. THIS WAS INSCRIBED IN THE BOOK OF RECORDS
BY ROYAL DECREE.

The verb *vayitalu* is difficult to translate and thus the method used to execute Bigthan
and Teresh is unclear. This word is also used later in the story to describe the execution of Haman and his sons. The root *talah* means ''to hang.'' Whether the condemned was hanged by the neck on a gallows or impaled on stakes, as was the
custom of the time, cannot be precisely determined by the text. After considerable
explanation, Koehler-Baumgartner (p. 1739) concludes that ''in Esther what is
primarily suggested is punishment by hanging on a gallows.'' The *Targum* is unusually

41

unhelpful in clarifying this point and translates *vayitalu* as *itzt'livu* from the root *tzlav*, which means "impale" or "hang." (This word can also mean "crucify.") Nevertheless, in helping us to understand the process that was undertaken, the *Targum* adds the phrase "that was continually read before the king" after "the book of records." Apparently, this took the form of a daily news briefing so that he could know all that transpired in his realm.

Drunkenness on Purim

While most people think that Judaism does not promote total abstinence from alcohol, there are many scholars who believe that we do not have the right to place into our bodies any substances, including alcohol, that are potentially harmful. Our bodies belong to God; they are only lent to us and are the sacred precincts for our souls. In addition, most scholars acknowledge the potential for chemicals to be abused and and to damage our bodies—something that is frowned upon by Jewish tradition.

According to the Talmud (Babylonian Talmud, *M'gillah* 7b), one should become so intoxicated on Purim that one cannot tell the difference between "cursing Haman" or "blessing Mordecai." This notion became so much a part of Jewish culture that Purim parties were called *adloyadah*—a collapse of the Aramaic for "until he didn't know." The Rabbis were clearly uncomfortable with such a notion. While they felt that they could not reject this instruction (since it was part of the oral law), numerous commentators sought to define it in such a way that one need only drink a small amount of alcohol to reach the required level of intoxication. Some say that we should drink until we fall asleep; in this way, no harm could be done to the drinker or anyone else.

Most religious authorities today recognize the importance of moderation, even on Purim. As Rabbi Mark Washofsky notes, "the Bible speaks in praise of wine as a substance that 'gladdens the human heart' (Ps. 104:15)" but also tells us "to beware of 'wine when it is red,' for its color and smoothness hide the reality that 'in the end, it bites like a snake' and distorts the workings of the human mind (Prov. 23:31–32)" (*Jewish Living* [New York: UAHC Press, 2001], p. 263).

Jehoiachin

Son of Jehoiakim and Nehushta, Jehoiachin was king of Judah and a contemporary of the prophet Jeremiah. While II Kings 24:8 notes that he began his reign at eighteen, II Chronicles 36:9 suggests that he was only eight. Nevertheless, scholars date his short reign of three months and ten days to 598 B.C.E. The Babylonians removed him from office when Zedekiah was named king (II Chronicles 36:9–10).

Y'hoshua ben Karcha

Rabbi Y'hoshua ben Karcha was a contemporary of Shimon ben Gamliel II (second century C.E.). Because of his signature bald head, he was called *karcha*. (In Modern Hebrew, *keirei-ach* means "bald." Thus, the one who is bald is called a *karcha*.)

Zerubbabel

Zerubbabel is an Assyrian-Babylonian name meaning "the seed of Babylon." He was the grandson of Jehoiachin and led the first group of Jews who returned from captivity in Babylon during the first year of Cyrus of Persia's reign. Zerubbabel is also known for laying the foundation of the Second Temple.

Eunuchs

The custom of employing eunuchs in royal households was common in the ancient world. The term "eunuch" refers to a man or boy who was a harem attendant or some kind of royal court functionary in Asia. The name is derived from the Greek word *eunoukhos* (a castrated man employed to take charge of women of a harem and act as a chamberlain).

GLEANINGS

The Archetype of Amalek

The archetype of Amalek is surely among the most powerful and persistent in the Jewish imagination. It is rooted, in part, in three verses, Deuteronomy 25:17–19: "Remember what Amalek did to you by the way, when you were coming out of Egypt. How he met you by the way, and smote the hindmost of you, all that were feeble in your rear, when you were faint and weary, and he feared not God. Therefore, it shall be when the Lord your God has given you rest from all your enemies round about, in the land which the Lord thy God gives you . . . that you shall blot out the remembrance of Amalek from under the heavens. . . ."

The Talmudic rabbis assigned those verses as the maftir, the final Torah reading, on the Shabbat before Purim—known as Shabbat Zakhor, for the first word, remember, in the verses. The reason for this is hardly mysterious: Rabbinic tradition explicitly identifies Haman as the descendant of Amalek. The craven attempt of Amalek to destroy the people Israel when we "were faint and weary" foreshadows the efforts of Haman to annihilate the Jews in the story of Esther. Our tradition identifies Amalek as the archetypical eternal enemy of the Jewish people, and Jewish literature from ancient times on routinely collapses all who would attack Israel as yerek Amalek— "an appendage of Amalek."

[But] the commandment to annihilate Amalek must be reserved for God. Only the Divine can fully remove Amalek from the world. Israel should never aspire to fulfill the Deuteronomic injunction to "blot out the remembrance of Amalek from under the heavens," for human power is always circumscribed, never absolute. . . . While the ability to eradicate evil and achieve absolute justice is reserved for God, even the Holy One will never bring about those ends in history. Perfection is reserved for an eschaton beyond time.

The wisdom and moderation inherent in these assertions are of particular import for each of us as we contemplate the meaning of the Amalek myth at this time in our history. The story of Amalek reminds us that evil irredeemably mars the human condition. Our world is flawed, and no one—Jew or non-Jew—can deny this truth. The commandment to destroy Amalek bids us combat evil. The rabbis adopted the metaphor of Amalek because the memory of Amalek promotes repair of the world.

At the same time, our commentators rendered the actual application of the Amalek paradigm historically inoperative. Instinctively and correctly, they recoiled from the absolutism and the danger of oversimplification that emerge from application of such a paradigm. The Talmudic rabbis understood that each generation is unique, and they did not want to collapse all future opponents into an ancient archetype. Assertions that identify our admittedly very real present-day foes as Amalek or yerek Amalek reduce our antagonists to dangerous caricatures. The rabbis erected a cautionary fence around the Amalek narratives that instructs the people Israel to be judicious as we go about the task of confronting evil. It is a prudent message of self-control and sobriety well worth heeding in our present situation.

David Ellenson, "The Amalek Decision," Jerusalem Report, March 24, 2003, 43

Yom Kippur and Purim

A hasidic saying declares in a paradoxical pun: *yom kippurim yom k'Purim.* Yom Kippur, the solemn day of atonement, is like Purim, the most boisterous of Jewish feasts. But in what way do these holy days resemble one another? The business of Yom Kippur is the confession of sin. Individually and communally, over and over we beat our breasts and recite exhaustive alphabetical lists of malefactions—everything from arrogance to xenophobia. We abstain from food, water, and sex from sundown to sundown. Late in the day, at the afternoon service, however, the carnivalesque bursts into our liturgy. With blood sugar at low ebb, and self-congratulation for our asceticism on the rise, we read what may be the funniest book of the Bible, Jonah: a whale that can swallow people but can't digest them, animals that repent in sackcloth and ashes, a plant that grows like Jack's magic beanstalk equipped with a worm that can chomp it down at one go, and in its midst, the world's briefest, most effective, most reluctant prophet, the prophet who does not want his hearers to repent. This book, Arnold Band suggests, is a parody, burlesquing other biblical stories and punning outrageously. And where is our first written source for the custom of reading Jonah on Yom Kippur? It is in Megillah 31b, the tractate of the Babylonian Talmud whose major topic is the laws of Purim.

45

On Purim, on the other hand, while we are joking and freely imbibing and wearing silly costumes, we read the Book of Esther, whose laughter is frequently undercut by mourning, dread, and violence. Traditionally, at certain points in the narration, its lively cantillation slides into the haunting melody in which the Book of Lamentations is chanted, suggesting the tenuousness of all escapes. Texts, as Ricoeur says, "explode the worlds of their authors." Our judgment and our laughter are dynamic responses altered by changes in the world, the community, and the self we bring to every reading or ritual enactment. Because of this, the text of Esther is changed for us by memories of the Holocaust, the story in which Haman won. Purim of 1994 and 1996 have changed our encounter with the text yet again. We now bring with us new memories, new massacres of innocents: the terrible celebration at the Cave of Machpelah in Hebron, where Baruch Goldstein reenacted upon the bodies of praying Muslims the revenge of the Jews of Persia upon their enemies; and the retaliatory murders of Israeli children costumed for Purim—two new manifestations of Yom Kippur in the midst of Purim. During the last bloody chapters of the megillah, the laughter that accompanies public readings of this bawdy book is silenced. Amid the uproar of the carnival, we are forced to recall that the reality and finality of death, the danger of vengeance, and the terrible repetition compulsion to which it shackles both victor and vanquished.

What kind of laughter will unite and transform us as audience and inheritors of classical texts? Not the laughter of separation and superiority, the laughter that says, "I could be a fool like you." Not ungenerous laughter. It would be ungenerous to regard the struggle for holiness, which was the conscious motivation of our storytellers, merely as a cloak for their unconscious struggle for hegemony. Surely the desire for the good, the desire for closeness for God, is as real and irreducible as the desire for power, even if we have a lot of trouble telling them apart. Simply holding the stories up to ridicule, stripping them of redemptive potential, does not effect the holy comedy we as audience must bring about.

Our understanding of judgment is challenged by every new discovery into human accountability. The more adept we become with our richer psychological language, and the more we appreciate all the subtle contingencies—biochemical, genetic, social, anthropological, psychological, and historical—that both constrain and enlarge our choices, the more bitter our tears and the deeper our indignation about the violence we have done and continue to do to those who are both like us and utterly other than ourselves. Our understanding of comedy must deepen as well. Being human, none of us can see very far. Our choices in this predicament are to help one another to clearer vision and to discover a delight in the absurdity of our errors or to break our hearts alone in the darkness. I choose to walk through stories searching for the waters of salvation: the hidden springs of laughter that well up once we are willing to relinquish the suffocating security of the dominator or the smoldering grudge of the victim. . . .

Rachel Adler, *Engendering Judaism: An Inclusive Theology and Ethics*
(Philadelphia: Jewish Publication Society of America, 1998), 17–19

A New Celebration of Revelation

The new rabbinic understanding of God's activity in history is reflected in the greatly increased importance ascribed to the Book of Esther. In early rabbinic times, there was controversy over whether it was divinely inspired (*Megillah* 7a). Modern biblical scholars, Jewish as well as Christian, have also sometimes felt uneasiness over the Book of Esther. In the talmudic period, however, there were those who placed it above the Prophets and other Writings, ranking it together with the Five Books of Moses. The Jerusalem Talmud states: "The truth of the Book of Esther is like the truth of the Torah . . . just as the Torah requires interpretation, so does the Book of Esther" (*Megillah* 1:1). Indeed, Esther is the only part of the Bible outside the Torah that is a subject of commentary in the Mishnah and the Talmud. The Jerusalem Talmud goes on to say:

> The Book of Esther was given to Moses on Sinai, but since there is no chronological order in the Torah, it appears after the Five Books of Moses. Rabbi Johanan said that the Prophets and the Writings will one day be annulled, but the words of the Torah will not. . . . Resh Lakish added that the Book of Esther will also never be invalidated. (*Megillah* 1:5)

In his *Mishneh Torah*, Maimonides ascribes the same degree of importance to Esther.

> All the books of the Prophets and all the Writings will be annulled in the days of the Messiah, except for the Book of Esther. It will continue to be binding like the Five Books of Moses and the entire oral law, which will never be invalidated. (*Hilkhot Megillah* 2:18)

These comparisons between the Torah and Esther can be explained in a simple way: the former encapsulates the manner in which history impressed itself upon the early Israelite community, but the latter accords better with the Jewish experience of history in the talmudic period and afterward. Instead of the Torah's picture of God intervening directly in the historical process and guiding His covenantal partners, Esther depicts history as an absurd drama in which intrigue, manipulation, and pure chance apparently determine whether the Jewish people will be preserved or destroyed. In their Midrashic analysis of Esther, however, the rabbis were able to discern a providential drama operating behind the scenes.

> "On that night, the king's sleep was shaken" [Esther 6:1]: heaven, the throne of the Supreme King of Kings, the Holy One, blessed be He, was shaken when He saw Israel in such distress. (*Esther Rabbah* 10:1)

Where others might see merely the foolish and jealous king of Persia unable to sleep, the rabbis perceived the miraculous awakening of God from His apparent slumber in order to save the Jews from destruction. Others might see merely the intrigues of the Persian court and Esther's sexual manipulations of Ahasuerus and Haman; the rabbis perceived the hidden hand of God working to turn the genocidal plan of Haman into a victory for the Jews over their enemies (*Megillah* 12a–17a). The absence of any direct reference to God in the Book of Esther, which is hardly accidental, made the book all the more relevant to the situation of the Jews in exile. Persons of mature covenantal faith, who could discover God's providential love in the story narrated, were able to feel God's commanding voice under all historical conditions. The spiritual power implicit in the Sinai covenant reached full expression when the Jewish community was able to trust in the covenantal promise despite the apparent arbitrariness of history. Accordingly, the rabbis taught that the acceptance of the covenant of Sinai was less strictly valid than its renewed assertion after the defeat of Haman, since in the latter circumstance there was no divine coercion.

...The full ratification of the covenantal relationship between God and Israel was consummated when the rabbis could interpret the narrated actions of Mordecai, Esther, and Ahasuerus as manifestations of God's redemptive involvement in history. In its treatment of the Book of Esther, the Talmud achieved the same liberation from literalism, the same transcendence of the written revealed word by the oral tradition, as it achieved in its Torah exegesis. What began at Sinai as an externally imposed system of norms had become a successful internalization of those norms when Purim was identified as the celebration of the free acceptance of the Torah.

David Hartman, A Living Covenant: The Innovative Spirit in Traditional Judaism
(Woodstock, VT: Jewish Lights Publishing, 1997), 17–20

ג:א אַחַר הַדְּבָרִים הָאֵלֶּה גִּדַּל הַמֶּלֶךְ אֲחַשְׁוֵרוֹשׁ אֶת־הָמָן בֶּן־
הַמְּדָתָא הָאֲגָגִי וַיְנַשְּׂאֵהוּ וַיָּשֶׂם אֶת־כִּסְאוֹ מֵעַל כָּל־הַשָּׂרִים אֲשֶׁר
אִתּוֹ:

3:1 AFTER THESE EVENTS, KING AHASUERUS HONORED
HAMAN, SON OF HAMMEDATHA THE AGAGITE, BY
PROMOTING HIM AND SETTING HIS SEAT HIGHER THAN
ANY OF THE OTHER MINISTERS.

The time period referred to by this verse is somewhat ambiguous. The *Targum* translates the word *d'varim* (which we translate as "events") as "conversation." The conversation, the *Targum* explains, takes place between God and the Attribute of Justice: "Having entered into the presence of God—the Master of the world—the Attribute of Justice declares, 'It is wicked Haman, of the seed of Agag, son of Amalek, he who went down from Shushan to Jerusalem to prevent the rebuilding of the Temple, who has now been promoted as master over all and has been seated higher than any other minister.' God responds, 'My verdict on him will not be proclaimed until he has reached high position and is known to all nations. Only then will he be punished for all the troubles that he and his fathers have brought to the people of the House of Israel.'"

Rashi identifies "these events" as the actions taken by Mordecai and Esther to save the king, which ultimately allow Israel to be saved. Although Haman is "promoted," the events leading to his downfall have already been set in motion. For Rashi, this is in keeping with the Rabbinic notion "God provides the remedy before the disease" (Babylonian Talmud, *M'gillah* 13b).

Ibn Ezra thinks that the time period for "these events" is five years. He also explains that "a seat higher than any of the other ministers" means that each of the ministers has his own throne in the palace. Thus, Haman's throne is higher than the rest.

גָּב וְכָל־עַבְדֵי הַמֶּלֶךְ אֲשֶׁר־בְּשַׁעַר הַמֶּלֶךְ כֹּרְעִים וּמִשְׁתַּחֲוִים לְהָמָן כִּי־כֵן צִוָּה־לוֹ הַמֶּלֶךְ וּמָרְדֳּכַי לֹא יִכְרַע וְלֹא יִשְׁתַּחֲוֶה:

3:2 BECAUSE IT WAS THE ROYAL DECREE, ALL THE KING'S SERVANTS AT THE PALACE GATE WOULD BOW AND PROSTRATE THEMSELVES BEFORE HAMAN. MORDECAI, HOWEVER, WOULD NEITHER KNEEL NOR PROSTRATE HIMSELF.

Haman's promotion entitles him to certain privileges and honors. People are to bow to Haman as they would the king. It would be too simple to suggest that Mordecai refuses to bow before Haman because, as a Jew, he will only bow before God; indeed, he would certainly be prepared to acknowledge the royal status of the king. The *Targum*, then, offers a suggestion as to why Mordecai chooses not to bow. It is not merely to Haman alone that the people are bowing. Rather, they are bowing to a statue that is also in the palace gate (literally, ''king's gate''). For Mordecai, bowing to a statue would constitute idol worship.

Rashi takes this notion a little further. He suggests that Haman has declared himself a deity. As a result, Mordecai could not bow. Ibn Ezra agrees with the *Targum* and suggests that Haman has symbols of idolatry attached to his hat. Thus, if Mordecai were to bow to Haman, it would be tantamount to idol worship.

Interestingly, by refusing to bow to Haman, Mordecai puts himself in danger, something that a Jew is forbidden to do, and puts his people in danger as well. The interpretations of the *Targum* and later Rabbinic literature provide justification for his actions. Later Jewish law established rules on martyrdom (which Mordecai would not have known): To save one's life, a Jew can do anything in public but engage in forbidden sexual relations, commit murder, or carry out idolatry.

ג:ג וַיֹּאמְרוּ עַבְדֵי הַמֶּלֶךְ אֲשֶׁר־בְּשַׁעַר הַמֶּלֶךְ לְמָרְדֳּכָי מַדּוּעַ אַתָּה
עוֹבֵר אֵת מִצְוַת הַמֶּלֶךְ:

3:3 THE KING'S SERVANTS WHO WERE AT THE PALACE GATE SAID TO MORDECAI, "WHY ARE YOU NOT OBEYING THE KING'S COMMANDS?"

It is not clear whether the king's servants are simply questioning Mordecai's actions or if they are warning him that his behavior is a direct refusal of the king's command. The *Targum* reminds us that the "king's gate" (the literal Hebrew) was the gate of the palace, so we have included this information in our translation.

ג:ד וַיְהִי כְּאָמְרָם אֵלָיו יוֹם וָיוֹם וְלֹא שָׁמַע אֲלֵיהֶם וַיַּגִּידוּ לְהָמָן
לִרְאוֹת הֲיַעַמְדוּ דִּבְרֵי מָרְדֳּכַי כִּי־הִגִּיד לָהֶם אֲשֶׁר־הוּא יְהוּדִי:

3:4 ALTHOUGH THEY WOULD SPEAK TO HIM EVERY DAY, HE WOULD NOT LISTEN TO THEM. SO THEY REPORTED HIM TO HAMAN TO SEE WHETHER MORDECAI'S WORDS WOULD STAND, FOR HE HAD TOLD THEM THAT HE WAS A JEW.

This verse reveals a great deal about Mordecai's behavior and his relationship to the king's palace guards. Apparently, as a nobleman, he frequently exchanged words with the guards, but in this case, the frequent exchange was a result of his defiance. In addition, he had not disclosed his Jewish identity. The author is probably intentionally punning the words "would stand" as a reference to Mordecai's refusal to bow to Haman.

The *Targum* contends that the antecedent for "would stand" is not clear, suggesting that it could refer to Haman or Mordecai. According to the *Targum*, Haman's words are that one should worship an idol even if it is of little worth. Mordecai's words are that Jews neither worship nor bow before an idol. Rashi confirms the *Targum*'s latter understanding, reading "would stand" as being attached to Mordecai's words. But Ibn Ezra wonders why Mordecai reveals his identity, since doing so places both himself and the entire Jewish community in danger. Perhaps Mordecai should have asked Esther to remove him from the palace gate so that his presence would not provoke Haman, who has risen to a powerful position. Mordecai could not just walk away from the situation because to leave the palace gate without permission of the king would place his life in danger as well.

ג: ה וַיַּרְא הָמָן כִּי־אֵין מָרְדֳּכַי כֹּרֵעַ וּמִשְׁתַּחֲוֶה לוֹ וַיִּמָּלֵא הָמָן חֵמָה:

3:5 When Haman saw that Mordecai would not kneel or prostrate himself before him, he [Haman] became filled with rage.

While this verse seems straightforward, the *Targum* does not want to let go of its insistence that there is an idol in the picture and therefore adds that it is "a statue" before which Mordecai would not kneel.

ג: ו וַיִּבֶז בְּעֵינָיו לִשְׁלֹחַ יָד בְּמָרְדֳּכַי לְבַדּוֹ כִּי־הִגִּידוּ לוֹ אֶת־עַם מָרְדֳּכָי וַיְבַקֵּשׁ הָמָן לְהַשְׁמִיד אֶת־כָּל־הַיְּהוּדִים אֲשֶׁר בְּכָל־מַלְכוּת אֲחַשְׁוֵרוֹשׁ עַם מָרְדֳּכָי:

3:6 When Haman found out who the people of Mordecai were, it did not seem enough just to kill him. He decided to destroy the people of Mordecai—all the Jews in the entire kingdom of Ahasuerus.

Haman had not known that Mordecai is Jewish, and he seems not to know the connection between Mordecai and Esther. It is clear that Haman is angry and vengeful. Nevertheless, with regard to Haman's feelings about Mordecai, it is difficult to fit the Hebrew idiom into an American English idiom. *Vayivez b'einav* literally means "it was despicable in his eyes." Koehler-Baumgartner (p. 117) suggests "he considered it beneath his dignity." We choose to render the phrase as "it did not seem enough," recognizing that the intensity of the Hebrew and Haman's subsequent actions seem much more intense than does the selected English idiom.

The *Targum* recognizes the severity of Haman's response to Mordecai's insubordination. It adds that Haman had been told that Mordecai was a descendant of Jacob—the progenitor of the Jews. Thus it became known that Mordecai's people had taken the birthright and the blessing from Esau (Genesis 25:19–28:22), who was Haman's ancestor.

ג:ז בַּחֹדֶשׁ הָרִאשׁוֹן הוּא־חֹדֶשׁ נִיסָן בִּשְׁנַת שְׁתֵּים עֶשְׂרֵה לַמֶּלֶךְ אֲחַשְׁוֵרוֹשׁ הִפִּיל פּוּר הוּא הַגּוֹרָל לִפְנֵי הָמָן מִיּוֹם לְיוֹם וּמֵחֹדֶשׁ לְחֹדֶשׁ שְׁנֵים־עָשָׂר הוּא־חֹדֶשׁ אֲדָר:

3:7 In the twelfth year of the reign of Ahasuerus, in the first month, the month of Nisan, in Haman's presence, *pur*, meaning "the lot," was cast to determine the month and the day. It fell out upon the twelfth month, the month of Adar.

While there is a great deal of debate as to what this *pur* actually is and how it relates to the name of the festival of Purim, it is clear that someone uses *purim* (plural of *pur*) to determine the fate of the Jewish people. Rashi notes that it is not clear who casts the lots. He suggests that the chosen "lot" actually indicates the day on which the action will be successfully completed. This differs from the understanding of many that it is about the day on which the action is to begin.

For Ibn Ezra, *pur* is a Persian word meaning "lot." He reports on one Rabbinic view that Haman chooses Adar because Moses died in that month, not knowing that Moses was also born in that month. This would imply a great deal of Jewish knowledge on behalf of Haman, which is unlikely. Rashi offers another view that the date is chosen based on astrological considerations—which seems more likely, especially when considering that the *purim*, probably stones, likely were used as a means of divining. Rashi's own thought is that the time is divinely chosen so that the Jews might repent and be saved from destruction.

ג:ח וַיֹּאמֶר הָמָן לַמֶּלֶךְ אֲחַשְׁוֵרוֹשׁ יֶשְׁנוֹ עַם־אֶחָד מְפֻזָּר וּמְפֹרָד בֵּין הָעַמִּים בְּכֹל מְדִינוֹת מַלְכוּתֶךָ וְדָתֵיהֶם שֹׁנוֹת מִכָּל־עָם וְאֶת־דָּתֵי הַמֶּלֶךְ אֵינָם עֹשִׂים וְלַמֶּלֶךְ אֵין־שֹׁוֶה לְהַנִּיחָם:

3:8 HAMAN THEN SAID TO KING AHASUERUS, "THERE IS A CERTAIN PEOPLE SCATTERED AND DISPERSED THROUGHOUT THE OTHER PEOPLES OF ALL THE PROVINCES OF YOUR KINGDOM WHOSE LAWS ARE DIFFERENT FROM ANY OTHER NATION AND WHO DO NOT KEEP THE KING'S LAWS. IT IS NOT IN YOUR INTEREST TO ALLOW THEM TO STAY.

For a modern reader, approaching the story of Esther against the backdrop of the Holocaust, Haman's words are especially chilling. These are Haman's introductory remarks. Only later will he say what he wants the king specifically to do with the Jewish community of ancient Persia. He does not mention his own anger—only that they are disobeying the laws of the king. He has not yet told the king that the people are Jewish, but he does know that Mordecai is Jewish. (See 3:1.) Neither he nor the king is aware that Esther is one of these people.

While it is true that the Jewish people have different laws, it is also true that they generally follow the king's laws. The Jewish people are, in fact, obligated by Jewish law to maintain the "law of the land," that is, the king's laws. In this story, however, Mordecai defies a royal order to bow before an officer of the court. Although we do not know Mordecai's exact motivation for refusing to bow down before Haman (with or without an accompanying statue), he may have considered the command to follow the "law of the land" and decided that it was more important to assert his belief in one God and not commit idol worship.

It is interesting to note that a Persian loanword is used here. The Persian word comes into Hebrew as *dat*, which underlies the word *data*, "law" (Koehler-Baumgartner, p. 234) as in *dateihem* (their laws) in this verse. The word continued to develop and now has come to mean "religion" in Modern Hebrew. In our translation, we follow what we consider to be the intention of Koehler-Baumgartner (p. 1437) in its translation of *shoveh*, "to be appropriate, to be in accordance with." We have supplied "your" as in "in your interest." We follow Koehler-Baumgartner (p. 680) in translating *l'hanicham* as "allow them to stay."

Rashi sees "the king's law" through the lens of tax collection for the king's service. He explains *ein shoveh* as "what benefit" rather than "not to your interest."

For Ibn Ezra, the notion of being scattered and separated from one another is a moral flaw, for such people leave their families and do not stick together. They had "different laws" and did not observe "the king's laws." Thus, they were unlike other peoples who did observe the laws. *Ein shoveh* then becomes "it is not fitting" or "it is not correct."

ג:ט אִם־עַל־הַמֶּלֶךְ טוֹב יִכָּתֵב לְאַבְּדָם וַעֲשֶׂרֶת אֲלָפִים כִּכַּר־כֶּסֶף אֶשְׁקוֹל עַל־יְדֵי עֹשֵׂי הַמְּלָאכָה לְהָבִיא אֶל־גִּנְזֵי הַמֶּלֶךְ:

3:9 "I<small>F IT PLEASE THE KING, LET AN ORDER BE ISSUED TO DESTROY THEM. I WILL THEN WEIGH OUT TEN THOU-SAND TALENTS OF SILVER TO THE OFFICIALS TO BE BROUGHT INTO THE TREASURIES OF THE KING.</small>"

Why would Haman have to pay the king for such an order to be issued? Perhaps it is a way of persuading him to issue the order, or an expression of appreciation for his doing so. Maybe it is in recognition of the taxes that would be lost were the people to be destroyed. The *Targum* adds a rhetorical question: "Who can count the six hundred thousand [talents of silver] that their ancestors took when they left the slavery of Egypt?" This implies that the Jewish community indeed has the funds.

ג:י וַיָּסַר הַמֶּלֶךְ אֶת־טַבַּעְתּוֹ מֵעַל יָדוֹ וַיִּתְּנָהּ לְהָמָן בֶּן־הַמְּדָתָא הָאֲגָגִי צֹרֵר הַיְּהוּדִים:

3:10 T<small>HE KING TOOK OFF THE SIGNET RING FROM HIS HAND AND GAVE IT TO HAMAN, SON OF HAMMEDATHA THE AGAGITE, THE ENEMY OF THE JEWS.</small>

The signet ring is a means to authenticate any order that Haman might give, especially if it is to be issued in written form. Rashi suggests that it gives Haman royal warrant for anything that he wants to do.

ג:יא וַיֹּאמֶר הַמֶּלֶךְ לְהָמָן הַכֶּסֶף נָתוּן לָךְ וְהָעָם לַעֲשׂוֹת בּוֹ כַּטּוֹב
בְּעֵינֶיךָ:

3:11 THE KING SAID TO HAMAN, "THE MONEY IS YOURS
AND THE PEOPLE ARE YOURS. DO WHAT YOU WANT."

While rejecting Haman's offer to compensate the king for the loss of funds to his
treasury—through taxes—the king affirmed Haman's right to take the property of the
people he intended to kill, the entire Jewish community.

ג:יב וַיִּקָּרְאוּ סֹפְרֵי הַמֶּלֶךְ בַּחֹדֶשׁ הָרִאשׁוֹן בִּשְׁלוֹשָׁה עָשָׂר יוֹם בּוֹ
וַיִּכָּתֵב כְּכָל־אֲשֶׁר־צִוָּה הָמָן אֶל אֲחַשְׁדַּרְפְּנֵי־הַמֶּלֶךְ וְאֶל־הַפַּחוֹת
אֲשֶׁר עַל־מְדִינָה וּמְדִינָה וְאֶל־שָׂרֵי עַם וָעָם מְדִינָה וּמְדִינָה
כִּכְתָבָהּ וְעַם וָעָם כִּלְשׁוֹנוֹ בְּשֵׁם הַמֶּלֶךְ אֲחַשְׁוֵרשׁ נִכְתָּב וְנֶחְתָּם
בְּטַבַּעַת הַמֶּלֶךְ:

3:12 ON THE THIRTEENTH DAY OF THE FIRST MONTH, THE
ROYAL SCRIBES WERE SUMMONED AT HAMAN'S
COMMAND, SO THAT AN ORDER WRITTEN IN KING
AHASUERUS'S NAME AND SEALED BY THE ROYAL SIGNET
BE SENT TO THE KING'S SATRAPS, TO THE GOVERNORS
OF EACH PROVINCE IN ITS OWN SCRIPT AND TO THE
OFFICIALS OF EACH PEOPLE IN ITS OWN LANGUAGE.

Haman intends to carry out the destruction of the Jews not by warfare or murderous
mob, but through the orderly mechanism of the government. This verse notes that the
order is to be sent out to all of the provinces in their local languages, so that there will
be no misunderstanding about the nature or extent of the decree.

The English word "satraps" is probably unfamiliar. It means "military governors"
and is the best direct translation of the word *achashdarp'nei*, which, according to
Koehler-Baumgartner (p. 37), has Old Persian and Greek roots, showing how professional terms and military ranks that indicate similar societal structures move from
one language to another.

Ibn Ezra (in his comment on v. 11) notes that the order for the destruction of the Jewish people is prepared on the thirteenth of Nisan. If this is so, the fast that Esther would proclaim (see 4:16) would have Mordecai fast on the first days of Passover. (Later, the entire community will fast. See 4:3.) However, Ibn Ezra continues, it is possible that the day of fasting was not widely known. He also notes that Haman is hanged in the month of Nisan. Ibn Ezra is attempting to explain the differences in dates. It is possible that the edict was not yet received in the outer provinces.

ג:יג וְנִשְׁלוֹחַ סְפָרִים בְּיַד הָרָצִים אֶל־כָּל־מְדִינוֹת הַמֶּלֶךְ לְהַשְׁמִיד לַהֲרֹג וּלְאַבֵּד אֶת־כָּל־הַיְּהוּדִים מִנַּעַר וְעַד־זָקֵן טַף וְנָשִׁים בְּיוֹם אֶחָד בִּשְׁלוֹשָׁה עָשָׂר לְחֹדֶשׁ שְׁנֵים־עָשָׂר הוּא־חֹדֶשׁ אֲדָר וּשְׁלָלָם לָבוֹז:

3:13 WRITTEN ORDERS WERE SENT BY COURIERS TO ALL THE PROVINCES OF THE KINGDOM TO DESTROY, TO KILL, AND TO MASSACRE ALL THE JEWS, YOUNG AND OLD, WOMEN AND CHILDREN, AND TO PLUNDER ALL THAT THEY HAD. THIS WAS TO HAPPEN IN ONE DAY, THE THIRTEENTH DAY OF THE TWELFTH MONTH OF ADAR.

If the massacre happened in one day, it would prevent any member of the Jewish community from hearing about the events until it was too late for them to do anything about it.

Rashi uses I Samuel 2:27 (*nigloh nigleiti*, "I revealed Myself") as a parallel in order to explain that although *v'nishloach* (were sent) is what grammarians call a *nifal*, "passive," infinitive, it is used here in an active sense. Ibn Ezra also refers readers to a passage in I Samuel, but to another verse (20:28, *nishol nishal David*, "David earnestly asked me") to explain how this *nifal* form can be used in an active sense.

ג:יד פַּתְשֶׁגֶן הַכְּתָב לְהִנָּתֵן דָּת בְּכָל־מְדִינָה וּמְדִינָה גָּלוּי לְכָל־הָעַמִּים
לִהְיוֹת עֲתִדִים לַיּוֹם הַזֶּה:

3:14 A COPY OF THE TEXT WAS PUBLISHED AS LAW IN EVERY
PROVINCE AND MADE KNOWN TO EVERY PEOPLE TO
PREPARE FOR THAT DAY.

Haman—through the king's edict—makes genocide legal. It follows governmental
enactments. Haman—as Hitler after him—seeks to destroy the Jewish people and to
do so "legally."

The *Targum* translates this verse literally. It translates *patshegen* (copy) with an
Aramaic loanword based on a Persian base of *ditagma*, which is a Greek loanword
underlying the contemporary English word "document." While Rashi also treats
patshegen as an Aramaic loanword, he explains it as *l'hinatein dat* (published as law).
This means that it reflects a royal command. Rashi also explains that *galui l'chol
haamim* (made known to every people) means that everyone knew it. Ibn Ezra takes
this word to mean "copy" and "known." For him, it suggests that this activity is not
done in secret.

ג:טו הָרָצִים יָצְאוּ דְחוּפִים בִּדְבַר הַמֶּלֶךְ וְהַדָּת נִתְּנָה בְּשׁוּשַׁן הַבִּירָה
וְהַמֶּלֶךְ וְהָמָן יָשְׁבוּ לִשְׁתּוֹת וְהָעִיר שׁוּשָׁן נָבוֹכָה:

3:15 AT THE KING'S COMMAND, THE COURIERS SPED OUT,
AND THE LAW WAS PROMULAGATED IN THE FORTRESS
OF SHUSHAN. HAMAN AND THE KING SAT DRINKING,
BUT THE CITY OF SHUSHAN WAS STUNNED.

An order to massacre a group of people is issued in a city filled with that people, and
those who issued the order are so bereft of feeling that they can sit and drink
nonchalantly. The city's inhabitants, however, are stunned by such actions. This may
indicate that the people of the city may not simply follow or support the decree.
Clearly, while Haman is able to use the law to make the genocide possible, he may
not have yet succeeded in demonizing the Jews in the eyes of the people of Shushan

to a degree that will allow it to be carried out. Genocide, whenever and wherever it is enacted, seems to require the deadening of human feeling and denial of the humanity of the intended victims. Perhaps, that is why the king and Haman are drinking— so that they can forget the humanity of those whose death they have just ordered. It is this type of disregard for humanity that provoked Shakespeare to place these words in the mouth of Shylock: "If you prick us, do we not bleed? If you tickle us, do we not laugh?"

While the *Targum* understands this verse otherwise literally, it translates the word *navochah* ("stunned," "perplexed," or "mixed up" in a colloquial sense) as *mitarb'lah* ("mixed" in a literal sense) to explain that the city of Shushan was "mixed with the rejoicing of the foreign peoples [at the anticipated massacre of the Jews]" and the "sound of the weeping of the people of the House of Israel."

Rashi explains that the phrase "the law was promulgated in the fortress of Shushan" indicates that the fortress is the king's residence and it is there that the law is first promulgated. He adds that the term "stunned" only applies to the part of the city of Shushan outside the area of the king's fortress.

Ibn Ezra agrees with Rashi. He points out that the only Jewish resident in the fortress of Shushan, which is filled with the king's courtiers, is Mordecai.

GLEANINGS

Evil

A man once stood before God, his heart breaking from the pain and injustice in the world. "Dear God," he cried out, "look at all the suffering, the anguish, and distress in Your world. Why don't You send help?"

God responded, "I did send help. I sent you."

I believe we are sent by God to conquer evil, soothe suffering, and create joy. When we reach out to people in pain, we do God's work. Why there needs to be pain and suffering in the first place is an understandable question but ultimately a pointless one. There are those who believe suffering is inflicted by God as punishment for sin. Others simply accept on faith that what seems like evil to us actually has a purpose in God's great plan, but being human means we can never fully appreciate its role. Then there are those who refuse to blame God for evil; they blame humanity instead. I am one of those. For me, for most of us, I suspect, God is not an omnipotent, supernatural power but a power manifest in humanity at its best. If this is so, then the answer to cruelty lies not in heaven but on earth. Salvation will come to us not from God above but from each other.

Steven Z. Leder, *The Extraordinary Nature of Ordinary Things*
(South Orange, NJ: Behrman House, 1999), 39–40.

Descent into Chaos

The Holocaust is the closing parenthesis for much of Jewish life; it kills the spirit as well as the body. Whoever enters the kingdom of night cannot emerge whole, cannot remain the same person but must be deeply transformed. And as much as all of humanity is affected, the Jew even more so: the remnant of Jewry that emerges from the war does so having been thrown and shaped and fired into new form. We who live after are different from those who came before.

For the Jew, the relationship with God, one's own self-identity as a member of this people, and the connection with the rest of humanity are fundamentally and

profoundly changed. One cannot be a Jew without being touched at the most fundamental level by images of the Holocaust. And insofar as being a Jew is a paradigm of
the larger human family, humanity itself is transformed. Good and evil, holy and
unholy, divinity and secularity all take on new colorations of meaning.

So much turned to smoke in that conflagration, so much disappeared, physically
and spiritually. From one perspective, the Holocaust is part of a continuum of perse-
cution in Jewish history. But that says too little, for tragically the Holocaust extends
beyond that history and confronts us with a new dimension. Here we are forced to
painfully say, "Would that the destruction had achieved only the level of the past," for
then so much and so many would have been saved.

Our generation has been forced to witness mass destruction on a previously un-
imagined scale; our conscious and our subconscious have not absorbed visions of
unparalleled evil.

Edward Feld, *The Spirit of Renewal: Crisis and Response in Jewish Life.*
(Woodstock, VT: Jewish Lights Publishing, 1991), 83–84

Jewish Enough

What has also been overlooked in the discussion of freedom as a threat to Jewish
survival is that it makes possible a new basis of Jewish continuity. Now that Jews are,
so to speak, no longer socially constrained to be Jews, they may, of course, choose to
give up their Jewishness. But the same freedom makes it possible for them to choose
to be Jewish in a new way—that is, to take up the fact of their birth and make it, upon
consideration, the personally willed basis of their existence. Their Jewishness now
becomes as much their decision as their parents' act and transforms the old familial
and social inertia of Jewish survival into an existential Jewish continuity in which the
self pledges its freedom to the millennial concerns of the Jewish people.

The potential virtues of such a free Jewishness may most easily be seen on the
psychological level. In adolescents and young adults, coercion often evokes rebellion.
Often it is not the substance of what is imposed that is resented, but the pressure.
Since adulthood and maturity in our time are associated with being free to make up
one's own mind, being allowed to decide against one's parents or society is a critical
right. And everyone feels oppressed insofar as he is not given legitimate scope in
which to exercise self-determination. A good deal of the youth rebellion is a struggle

for such independence—and I think, the basis of the adult malaise centered about the question, Why am I living this way?

If being Jewish is only something forced upon me, it may have to be resisted simply as a part of trying to be one's own man. Since Jewishness carries with it special minority burdens and responsibilities, it is easy to reject Jewishness in the name of autonomy. In a society prating about freedom I do not think this is an insignificant danger. Moreover, if the emphasis on personal freedom grows in the United States, as I think it will, the importance of willing to be a Jew will increase. Obviously, not everyone in America is involved in expanding personal freedom; and in addition, traditional Judaism, like the rest of man's cultural and spiritual experience, did not, until recently, have this high estimate of man's autonomy. So there will be a good part of the Jewish community that will continue to do more or less what its parents did. But, with the overwhelming majority of Jews college-trained, urban sophisticates, the impact on them of the cultural emphasis on enhancing personal liberty should be substantial. Hence the new possibility of affirming one's Jewishness as a matter of self-determination is a valuable option in the new psychosocial situation in which Jews find themselves.

Eugene Borowitz, *The Masks Jews Wear*
(New York: Simon and Schuster, 1973), 48–49

CHAPTER FOUR

ד:א וּמָרְדֳּכַי יָדַע אֶת־כָּל־אֲשֶׁר נַעֲשָׂה וַיִּקְרַע מָרְדֳּכַי אֶת־בְּגָדָיו וַיִּלְבַּשׁ
שַׂק וָאֵפֶר וַיֵּצֵא בְּתוֹךְ הָעִיר וַיִּזְעַק זְעָקָה גְדוֹלָה וּמָרָה:

4:1 When Mordecai found out what happened, he
ripped his clothes, put on sackloth and ashes,
and went through the city crying out loudly
and bitterly.

The text doesn't indicate how Mordecai finds out about the edict. His response is to perform traditional acts of mourning (Ezek. 27:30; Gen. 37:34; Jonah 3:6). The *Targum* embellishes the verse by suggesting that Mordecai learned "through Elijah the High Priest what had occurred on High [in the Heavens] and how the Jewish people had been condemned to be destroyed because they had participated in and had been moved to lust by the feast held by the wicked King Ahasuerus. The Master of the universe sent Elijah the High Priest to tell Mordecai to arise and pray for his people. Upon hearing this, Mordecai ripped his clothes, put sackcloth on his body, ashes on his head, gave out a great cry, and wept with the bitterness of his soul in a sad voice."

Rashi tells us that Mordecai learns about Haman's plan and the edict to destroy the Jewish community in a dream. In that dream, Mordecai also learns the reason for the action: as punishment for the Jewish people bowing to idols during the time of Nebuchadnezzar. In addition, they had apparently derived (an unspecified) benefit from the feast of Ahasuerus. The tradition argues against eating with idol worshippers or "marrying their daughters," both of which are said to lead the individual astray. The Jews should not have gone to that meal in the first place.

ד:ב וַיָּבוֹא עַד לִפְנֵי שַׁעַר־הַמֶּלֶךְ כִּי אֵין לָבוֹא אֶל־שַׁעַר הַמֶּלֶךְ בִּלְבוּשׁ

שָׂק:

4:2 HE ONLY WENT UP TO THE KING'S GATE BECAUSE ONE COULD NOT ENTER THE KING'S GATE WEARING SACKCLOTH.

The text clarifies the previous verse: Why doesn't Mordecai go directly to Esther—even after his immediate response of putting on sackcloth and ashes? Because it would be inappropriate to enter the king's gate dressed in such a manner—and the guards would not allow him to enter in any case. So Mordecai only approaches the gate and does not attempt to enter through it into the king's residence.

ד:ג וּבְכָל־מְדִינָה וּמְדִינָה מְקוֹם אֲשֶׁר דְּבַר־הַמֶּלֶךְ וְדָתוֹ מַגִּיעַ אֵבֶל גָּדוֹל לַיְּהוּדִים וְצוֹם וּבְכִי וּמִסְפֵּד שַׂק וָאֵפֶר יֻצַּע לָרַבִּים:

4:3 WHEN THE KING'S LEGAL DIRECTIVE REACHED EVERY PROVINCE, THERE WAS GREAT MOURNING AMONG THE JEWS; MANY LAY IN SACKCLOTH AND ASHES. THERE WAS FASTING, WEEPING, AND OTHER RITES [WERE UNDERTAKEN].

While this is a straightforward verse, it is difficult to translate. As we learned in 3:13, the evil decree has been sent to all the provinces in the kingdom. This verse tells us what happens when it reaches each province. As a presentiment of their own death, the Jews initiate the mourning process. The verse continues by providing the reader with some details as to the specific rites of mourning undertaken. When Mordecai first learns of the decree (4:1), he puts on sackcloth and ashes. Other Jews react the same way. Still others weep and fast. Here we encounter a challenge in translation. While Koehler-Baumgartner (p. 607) translates *mispeid* as "funeral ceremony" or "mourning rites," the infinitive form (*lispod*) of the root *s-p-d* is used in the story of the burial of Sarah (Genesis 23:2), where the sense of the root is more than "to mourn." In the Genesis passage, it clearly indicates some sort of ritualized behavior to express that mourning. Since the text does not make these rites clear, we translate it as "other rites."

The *Targum* amplifies the verse by adding "in each city" to "every province" and "great righteous persons" to the "many [who] lay in sackcloth."

Rashi tells us that as soon as the messengers reached a particular city, the edict was put into force—even if the people had yet to take action against the Jews. Ibn Ezra adds that Mordecai was reciting *kinot*, liturgical mourning poems.

ד:ד וַתָּבוֹאנָה נַעֲרוֹת אֶסְתֵּר וְסָרִיסֶיהָ וַיַּגִּידוּ לָהּ וַתִּתְחַלְחַל הַמַּלְכָּה
מְאֹד וַתִּשְׁלַח בְּגָדִים לְהַלְבִּישׁ אֶת־מָרְדֳּכַי וּלְהָסִיר שַׂקּוֹ מֵעָלָיו
וְלֹא קִבֵּל:

4:4 WHEN ESTHER'S MAIDS AND EUNUCHS CAME AND TOLD HER, THE QUEEN FILLED WITH FEAR. SHE SENT CLOTHES FOR MORDECAI TO PUT ON SO THAT HE COULD TAKE OFF HIS SACKCLOTH, BUT HE WOULD NOT DO SO.

Perhaps Esther misunderstands why Mordecai is dressed in sackcloth and ashes. Maybe she is embarrassed to see him this way and offers him clothing for her sake more than his. Perhaps she is afraid that others might see him as well. It is also possible that she is fearful that a guard will take Mordecai for a beggar and harm him. Perhaps Esther knows about the edict (since the entire country was informed, according to 3:14–15) and feels that Mordecai is overreacting. As queen, perhaps she feels that she would be able to deal with it herself and so protect Mordecai from any harm. As we will see at the end of this chapter, it will take a strong statement from Mordecai to get Esther to come to her senses, realize the full potential impact of the edict, and use her influence with the king to protect the Jewish people.

ד:ה וַתִּקְרָא אֶסְתֵּר לַהֲתָךְ מִסָּרִיסֵי הַמֶּלֶךְ אֲשֶׁר הֶעֱמִיד לְפָנֶיהָ
וַתְּצַוֵּהוּ עַל־מָרְדֳּכָי לָדַעַת מַה־זֶּה וְעַל־מַה־זֶּה:

4:5 ESTHER SUMMONED HATHACH, ONE OF THE EUNUCHS
WHOM THE KING HAD ASSIGNED TO SERVE HER, AND
SENT HIM TO MORDECAI TO FIND OUT WHAT WAS
WRONG AND WHY [IT WAS TROUBLING HIM].

The speculation over Esther's action is resolved in this verse. Apparently, she has no idea why Mordecai is dressed in sackcloth and ashes. This could be so even if she knows about the king's directive to destroy the Jewish people of Persia if she is unfamiliar with the custom of dressing that way to gain divine intervention.

The *Targum* is interested in further identifying Hathach, since he has not been previously mentioned. For the *Targum*, the eunuch is Daniel (the Book of Daniel is set in the sixth century B.C.E., a chronological anomaly that does not trouble the *Targum*). According to the *Targum*, Daniel received the name Hathach "because by his words royal matters were decided [a play on the word 'decided,' *mit'chat'chan*]." In its translation, the *Targum* expands the text as follows: "Esther commanded Hathach to ask Mordecai why he was weeping and why he would not put on the royal apparel that she had sent."

ד:ו וַיֵּצֵא הֲתָךְ אֶל־מָרְדֳּכָי אֶל־רְחוֹב הָעִיר אֲשֶׁר לִפְנֵי שַׁעַר־הַמֶּלֶךְ:

4:6 SO HATHACH WENT TO SPEAK TO MORDECAI AT THE
PLAZA IN FRONT OF THE PALACE GATE.

Following the *Targum*, we add "to speak" after "went" and have rendered *shaar hamelech* (literally, "the king's gate") as "the palace gate." Since the *Targum* translates the word *r'chov* ("broad place" or, in Modern Hebrew, "street") as *p'taah* (wide open place), we translate it as "plaza."

ד:ז וַיַּגֶּד־לוֹ מָרְדֳּכַי אֵת כָּל־אֲשֶׁר קָרָהוּ וְאֵת פָּרָשַׁת הַכֶּסֶף אֲשֶׁר אָמַר הָמָן לִשְׁקוֹל עַל־גִּנְזֵי הַמֶּלֶךְ בַּיְּהוּדִים לְאַבְּדָם:

4:7 MORDECAI TOLD HIM EVERYTHING THAT HAD HAPPENED TO HIM AND ABOUT THE SUM OF MONEY THAT HAMAN HAD PROMISED TO DISPENSE TO THE ROYAL TREASURIES FOR THE DESTRUCTION OF THE JEWS.

While it may seem unusual that Mordecai would relate everything to a servant, it seems he does so because he wants to make sure that Esther learns everything. The *Targum* explains that "everything that had happened to" Mordecai was a result of Mordecai's "refusal to bow down to Haman or prostrate himself to the idol." The *Targum* also includes the precise amount of ten thousand talents (see 3:9) that Haman promised the keepers of the treasury "for the destruction of the Jews." For Rashi, the use of the familiar term *parashat* (sum of) in this context means a specific amount. However, Ibn Ezra translates *parashat* as "explanation," that is, Haman's explanation to the princes regarding what he wants for his money: not only the destruction of the Jews but the total obliteration of the Jewish people—genocide.

ד:ח וְאֶת־פַּתְשֶׁגֶן כְּתָב־הַדָּת אֲשֶׁר־נִתַּן בְּשׁוּשָׁן לְהַשְׁמִידָם נָתַן לוֹ לְהַרְאוֹת אֶת־אֶסְתֵּר וּלְהַגִּיד לָהּ וּלְצַוּוֹת עָלֶיהָ לָבוֹא אֶל־הַמֶּלֶךְ לְהִתְחַנֶּן־לוֹ וּלְבַקֵּשׁ מִלְּפָנָיו עַל־עַמָּהּ:

4:8 HE [MORDECAI] GAVE HIM [HATHACH] A COPY OF THE TEXT OF THE ORDER FOR THEIR [THE JEWISH PEOPLE'S] DESTRUCTION THAT HAD BEEN PUBLISHED IN SHUSHAN, TO SHOW TO ESTHER AND TO TELL HER TO GO TO THE KING, APPEAL TO HIM, AND PLEAD WITH HIM FOR HER PEOPLE.

Mordecai tells Hathach exactly what he wants Esther to do, trusting that he will relate his words to her. We translate the words *k'tav hadat* here as "the text of the order" rather than the literal "text of the law," even though the orders of the king become law once they are decreed. Note that the author chooses to emphasize the severity of the situation, and Mordecai's desperation, by using the progression of words "to tell," "to bid" (which we have not translated), "to appeal," and "to plead." Ibn Ezra tells us that the reason that Shushan is mentioned as the place of the first decree is because the majority of its population was Jewish.

ד:ט וַיָּבוֹא הֲתָךְ וַיַּגֵּד לְאֶסְתֵּר אֵת דִּבְרֵי מָרְדֳּכָי:

4:9 HATHACH WENT TO ESTHER AND TOLD HER WHAT
MORDECAI SAID.

Hathach follows Mordecai's instructions exactly and repeats to Esther what Mordecai told him.

ד:י וַתֹּאמֶר אֶסְתֵּר לַהֲתָךְ וַתְּצַוֵּהוּ אֶל־מָרְדֳּכָי:

4:10 ESTHER THEN GAVE THE FOLLOWING MESSAGE TO
HATHACH FOR MORDECAI:

It isn't clear why Esther does not just go to the palace gate and speak to Mordecai directly. Perhaps she does not want to raise any suspicion or place him or herself in any additional danger, especially since at this point no one (except Hatach) is aware of her Jewish background. The *Targum* expands the message given to Mordecai: he should not incite controversy with Haman, because Jacob and Esau had reconciled (see Genesis 33). According to Rabbinic tradition, Haman, son of Hammedatha the Agagite, was understood to be a descendant of the Amalekite king Agag and therefore an Amalekite, the enemy of Israel (see Esther 3:10). The Amalekites are considered descendants of Esau (see Genesis 36:12 and comment to Esther 3:1).

ד:יא כָּל־עַבְדֵי הַמֶּלֶךְ וְעַם־מְדִינוֹת הַמֶּלֶךְ יֹדְעִים אֲשֶׁר כָּל־אִישׁ וְאִשָּׁה
אֲשֶׁר יָבוֹא־אֶל־הַמֶּלֶךְ אֶל־הֶחָצֵר הַפְּנִימִית אֲשֶׁר לֹא־יִקָּרֵא אַחַת
דָּתוֹ לְהָמִית לְבַד מֵאֲשֶׁר יוֹשִׁיט־לוֹ הַמֶּלֶךְ אֶת־שַׁרְבִיט הַזָּהָב
וְחָיָה וַאֲנִי לֹא נִקְרֵאתִי לָבוֹא אֶל־הַמֶּלֶךְ זֶה שְׁלוֹשִׁים יוֹם:

4:11 "ALL THE KING'S SERVANTS AND ALL THE PEOPLE OF THE PROVINCES KNOW THAT IF ANY PERSON, MAN OR WOMAN, ENTERS THE INNER COURT, IN THE KING'S PRESENCE, WITHOUT BEING SUMMONED, THERE IS ONLY ONE LAW FOR HIM [OR HER]—THAT HE [OR SHE] BE PUT TO DEATH. THERE IS ONLY ONE EXCEPTION: IF THE KING EXTENDS HIS GOLDEN SCEPTER, THEN THAT PERSON MAY LIVE. AS FOR ME, I HAVE NOT BEEN SUMMONED TO COME TO THE KING FOR THE LAST THIRTY DAYS."

Now the reader finds out—in part—why Hathach has to serve as a go-between for Mordecai and Esther. This verse also sets up Esther's hesitation to take the information immediately to the king. She is concerned that he has not called for her (that is, for sexual relations, euphemistically emphasized by the author's use of the king's "golden scepter") in thirty days. Esther is concerned that the king is no longer interested in her. If so, she may be in danger and is certainly in no position to ask for the king to rescind his order, especially if he stands to gain financially from it.

The *Targum* expands the translation of the verse, in an effort to explain the nuances of the law: "Then Esther placed the following words in the mouth of Hathach and said to him, 'This is what you should say to Mordecai: Wicked Haman ordered, using the authority of Ahasuerus, that no one may enter the inner court, in the king's presence, without permission. Thus, all servants and all peoples dwelling in the provinces know that any man or woman who enters the inner court or approaches the king without being summoned by Haman, there is only one law—death, unless the king extended his golden scepter. And I have not been summoned to appear before the king for the last thirty days.'"

Ibn Ezra explains that the phrase "the people of the provinces" is used to indicate that even the uneducated people knew about this law. He explains that "there is only one law" means that there is only one law for all people.

ד:יב וַיַּגִּידוּ לְמָרְדֳּכָי אֵת דִּבְרֵי אֶסְתֵּר:

4:12 WHEN HE [H**ATHACH**] TOLD **M**ORDECAI WHAT **E**STHER

     HAD SAID,

This verse leads directly to the verse that follows. Again, the *Targum* expands its translation of the verse, but it is unclear why the *Targum* chooses to do so in this way: "When wicked Haman saw that Hathach, whose name was Daniel, entered and spoke to Esther, he became enraged and killed him [Hathach]. The angels Michael and Gabriel happened to be there. It was they who reported the words of Esther to Mordecai."

ד:יג וַיֹּאמֶר מָרְדֳּכַי לְהָשִׁיב אֶל־אֶסְתֵּר אַל־תְּדַמִּי בְנַפְשֵׁךְ לְהִמָּלֵט
בֵּית־הַמֶּלֶךְ מִכָּל־הַיְּהוּדִים:

4:13 MORDECAI SENT THIS MESSAGE TO **E**STHER: "**D**ON'T

     IMAGINE THAT BY BEING IN THE KING'S HOUSE YOU,

     MORE THAN ANY OTHER **J**EW, WILL ESCAPE.

Perhaps Mordecai is anticipating Esther's response. Maybe he is speaking from the experience of having raised her. Or perhaps he believes that this is the posture she is assuming, since she did not come herself to deliver the message. According to the *Targum*, Mordecai sends a message through the angels Michael and Gabriel. The *Targum* wants to make it clear that since Hathach is dead, the angels have to carry the message. Further, if Esther goes to the king, she has to go to save the people, not just herself.

ד:יד כִּי אִם־הַחֲרֵשׁ תַּחֲרִישִׁי בָּעֵת הַזֹּאת רֶוַח וְהַצָּלָה יַעֲמוֹד לַיְּהוּדִים מִמָּקוֹם אַחֵר וְאַתְּ וּבֵית־אָבִיךְ תֹּאבֵדוּ וּמִי יוֹדֵעַ אִם־לְעֵת כָּזֹאת הִגַּעַתְּ לַמַּלְכוּת:

4:14 "IF YOU KEEP QUIET NOW, LIBERATION AND DELIVER-
ANCE WILL COME FOR THE JEWS SOME OTHER WAY,
BUT YOU AND YOUR ANCESTOR'S HOUSE WILL PERISH.
WHO KNOWS, PERHAPS FOR A TIME SUCH AS THIS YOU
HAVE BECOME PART OF ROYALTY."

Mordecai remains guardedly optimistic and is clearly trying to persuade Esther to use the influence on the king that he believes she still possesses. This verse also raises an intriguing and powerful concept about providence. As Rabbi Lawrence Kushner once remarked, "God places you where you are supposed to be. And if you aren't sup-posed to be there, don't worry, you won't be there very long."

We have followed Ibn Ezra in translating *mimakom acheir* (literally "from another place") as "some other way." While many readers may recognize *makom* as a euphemism for God, as in *HaMakom*, "the Place," Ibn Ezra notes in the introduction to his commentary on the Book of Esther that God is not mentioned at all in the Book of Esther. He rejects the attempt to understand *makom* as a divine name. Although Rabbinic literature does use the word in this manner, Ibn Ezra points out that it is not used this way anywhere in biblical literature.

Although we follow Koehler-Baumgartner (p. 1197) in translating *revach* as "liberation," the word suggests the opening of a space, as *tzarah* (trouble) suggests the pressing in and the closing of space. Perhaps "ease" would be an alternative trans-lation of the word.

The *Targum* tells us why "liberation and deliverance will come for the Jews." In its translation, the *Targum* explains that "because of the eternal merit of the ancestors, God will save them from the power of their enemies." Then it adds, "But you and the tribe of your ancestors will perish because of that sin. Who is so wise as to know whether in the coming year you will still have royal status in such a situation?"

Rashi follows the *Targum* in explaining the meaning of "who knows" as "whether in the coming year, at the time when the massacre will occur, the king will still desire you." For Rashi, "part of royalty" refers to Esther's current status and not what it might be in the future.

In accordance with Ibn Ezra's previous comment regarding the absence of God in the story of Esther, he explains that deliverance will come from some human agency rather than from God. He takes the remainder of the verse literally: "If you think that you will escape, you will perish along with your father's house." Ibn Ezra explains "who knows" as "it may be that the only reason that you have reached the level of royalty at this time is that you might save the people of Israel."

ד:טו וַתֹּאמֶר אֶסְתֵּר לְהָשִׁיב אֶל־מָרְדֳּכָי:

4:15 ESTHER SENT THE FOLLOWING REPLY TO MORDECAI:

This verse is connected to the verse that follows. Just as the *Targum* suggests that the angels Michael and Gabriel carried Mordecai's message to Esther (4:13), it contends that these angels are also the carriers of Esther's response to Mordecai in this verse.

ד:טז לֵךְ כְּנוֹס אֶת־כָּל־הַיְּהוּדִים הַנִּמְצְאִים בְּשׁוּשָׁן וְצוּמוּ עָלַי וְאַל־
תֹּאכְלוּ וְאַל־תִּשְׁתּוּ שְׁלֹשֶׁת יָמִים לַיְלָה וָיוֹם גַּם־אֲנִי וְנַעֲרֹתַי
אָצוּם כֵּן וּבְכֵן אָבוֹא אֶל־הַמֶּלֶךְ אֲשֶׁר לֹא־כַדָּת וְכַאֲשֶׁר אָבַדְתִּי
אָבָדְתִּי:

4:16 "GO AND GATHER ALL THE JEWS WHO ARE IN SHUSHAN AND FAST FOR ME FOR THREE DAYS. DON'T EAT OR DRINK DURING THE DAY OR AT NIGHT. MY MAIDS AND I WILL FAST AS WELL. AFTERWARDS, ALTHOUGH IT IS AGAINST THE LAW, I WILL GO TO THE KING. IF I PERISH, I PERISH."

Finally the Esther we have been waiting for emerges. She is willing to reclaim her Jewish identity and put her life at risk for doing so. This is perhaps the point at which Esther truly becomes Hadassah.

The *Targum* makes the following additions to its translation of this verse. To the things which the Jews should do, it adds "pray to God." And to what Esther plans to do herself, it makes these additions: "I will perish from the harem," "as I was moved by force from you," and "for the sale of the salvation of the people of the House of Israel I will perish from this life." These statements all serve to bolster the argument that Esther never lost her connection or commitment to the Jewish people and was forced into the king's harem against her will.

Since readers may wonder what was actually against the law Esther is referring to in this verse, Rashi tells us that it was against the law to enter the king's presence, that is, to approach him without his consent or request. So Rashi emphasizes this verse in order to point out that this is a voluntary action on Esther's part. Previously she had been forced to appear before the king. In order to make wordplay out of Esther's last statement, Rashi explains *v'chaasher avadti avadti*, "If I perish, I perish," as "As I was lost from my father's house and lost from you; now that I will willingly have sexual relations with Ahasuerus, I will be dead to you."

To make the timing fit, Ibn Ezra suggests that Esther's "three days" of fasting is really two days and two nights. Otherwise, the day on which Haman is to act will come before the three days of fasting is over. He also tells us that this action shows that Esther trusts God more than she trusts her own beauty to get her through this situation, since fasting three days would undermine her beauty.

ד:יז וַיַּעֲבֹר מָרְדֳּכָי וַיַּעַשׂ כְּכֹל אֲשֶׁר־צִוְּתָה עָלָיו אֶסְתֵּר:

4:17 So Mordecai went out and did all that Esther had instructed him to do.

Because the word *vayaavor* (went out) can also mean "transgress," the *Targum* adds these words to its translation: "Troubled Mordecai entered and transgressed the joy of the Festival of Passover and decreed a fast and sat upon ashes and did all that Esther told him to do."

Rashi also picks up this meaning of *vayaavor* and tells readers that Mordecai transgressed the law by fasting on the first day of Passover, since Esther fasted and instructed others to fast for three days, which would be the fourteenth, fifteenth, and sixteenth of Nisan.

Rending a Garment

The custom of rending or tearing the garment of a mourner (known as *k'riah* in Hebrew) is found in the Bible and has been a salient custom of mourning throughout Jewish history. It is the ritualizing of an understandable emotional response to the news that a loved one has died. When Jacob sees Joseph's bloodstained coat, brought to him by his other sons, who tell Jacob that Joseph has been killed by a wild beast, Jacob reacts by tearing his garment (Genesis 37:34). Similarly, David tears his clothes when he hears of the death of King Saul (II Samuel 1:11). And in the Book of Job, Job is described as tearing his mantle when he begins to mourn the loss of his children (Job 1:20). The adoption of various acts of mourning have been used historically by Jews, particularly in the Bible (Numbers 14:6, Jonah 3:5), as a way of beseeching God to intervene and change what portends to have negative consequences for the Jewish people.

Sackcloth and Ashes

A mourner sits on the ground (hence, ashes or dirt) and avoids wearing comfortable clothing, such as the wearing of leather-soled shoes. Sackcloth is roughly woven cloth that is uncomfortable to wear. Thus, mourners in the Bible donned sackcloth and ashes. As with rending one's garments, these were considered to be acts of petition to persuade God to intervene and save the Jewish people from impending misfortune.

Fasting

While fasting is not a traditional ritual of mourning, it has always been a vehicle through which Jews burden (and even afflict) themselves in order to communicate to God recognition of their wrongdoings and their willingness to change. It is also a way of raising the individual from a mundane, material plane to one of the spirit. Thus, in the Book of Esther, it is one of several activities (in addition to the donning of sackcloth and ashes and the rending of garments) that reflect a desire on the part of the Jewish community of ancient Persia to try to escape the king's fatal decree.

Kinot

Kinot are best described as elegies or liturgical dirges, often associated with Tishah B'Av, where an entire collection is used to supplement and incorporate the regular liturgy. The *kinot* are chanted in the same melody as Lamentations, the biblical scroll designated to be read that day. Many of them were written after the Crusades and the Spanish Inquisition. The content of this poetry expresses the optimism, colored somewhat by disillusion, in the people's search for a reason for their suffering. They are girded by an underlying trust in God. Many of the *kinot* are written in a familiar acrostic or altered acrostic form, drawing their images from both the Talmud and midrashic literature.

GLEANINGS

Purim as a Model for Redemption and Rebirth

Purim is the holiday for the post-Holocaust world; it is a model for the experience of redemption in the rebirth of Israel. In this era, too, the redemption is flawed—by the narrow escape, by the great loss of life, by the officially "irreligious" nature of the leadership, by the mixed motives and characters of those who carried it out, by the human suffering it brought in its wake, and by the less-than-perfect society of Israel. In our time, too, the "purists" wait for a "supernatural" miracle. Some object because of the religiously nonobservant element; others are crushed by the morally disturbing Arab refugee problem. Just as doctrinaire feminists get hung up on the "feminine" techniques of Esther, so are ideologues put off by the moral compromises involved in Israel's alliances and by the fact that it now gets support from the Establishment. People preoccupied with the equivocal details miss the overriding validity of the Purim and Israel events, events which occurred when the moral condition of the world needed such redemption, almost at all costs. Similarly, the Martin Luthers of the world are embarrassed by religious miracles that cost blood, so they question the fundamental validity of any divine but all too human redemption. The people, Israel, knew then and now better. In an imperfect world, one must be grateful for partial redemption. Celebration inspires the people to perfect that redemption.

Irving Greenberg, The Jewish Way: Living the Holidays
(New York; Simon & Schuster, 1988), 251

The Problem of Purim

Purim is surely one of the most delightful holidays on the calendar.... But there is also a very serious side of Purim.... Purim is a memorial observance of attempted genocide. For a generation growing up in the ashes of Auschwitz, there is nothing amusing about attempted genocide. And most of us remember 1996 (5756) when terrorists murdered our children in their Purim costumes in Jerusalem.

How then can we celebrate Purim with mirth? The obvious answer is that we are celebrating the *failure* of the genocide attempt. If our happiness is in proportion to the stakes involved, then Purim rightly is one of our most joyous celebrations.

Correct as this answer may be, it doesn't fully take into account the depths of feeling associated with the somber side of our brush with national destruction.

Purim elicits two strongly conflicting yet sincerely heartfelt emotions. We are horrified at the attempted destruction of our people, but we are overjoyed that the attempt failed.

At the same time, we must reflect on the other problem with Purim—the violent rampage of revenge our ancestors wreaked against their neighbors (at least according to the Megilla). It was this account that tipped the mental imbalance of the Jewish man who committed the massacre in Hebron at Purim in 1994. Even if Purim is supposed to be a farce, it is now harder to find it amusing.

For this reason, the mirthful celebration of Purim by itself would be almost offensive. That is why we observe the Fast of Esther, *Taanit Ester*, the day before Purim. (When Purim occurs on Sunday, the Fast is observed on the previous Thursday.) From the morning until afternoon or evening, we observe a half-day fast, just as Esther observed a fast when the fate of her people hung in the balance. When we observe the Fast of Esther we solemnly commit ourselves to making a world where genocide is unknown, where all people enjoy their God-given human rights.

I believe that it is psychologically and spiritually crucial for us to observe both sides of Purim. We need—and perhaps deserve—the joyous celebration of Purim. But we also need the serious side of Purim. And that is the Fast of Esther, a day of somber reflection and action against war and genocide.

Jon-Jay Tilsen, http://www.beki.org/purim/html

Crossing the Vistula

I am usually the first faculty member to arrive at the college where I teach on Thursday mornings, so I was delighted and surprised to also find there the man who, for many years, has been my teacher. It was a brutally cold day and the windchill had turned the canyons of Manhattan into tundra. There we were, I in my high-tech down parka and he is an ankle-length fur coat and Russian hat. Since he had always been drawn to eccentric outfits, I was not surprised. The last time I had invited him to speak to my congregation, he showed up in a green, plaid sports jacket. When I gave him a quizzical glance, he explained that when he saw it on the rack it had whispered, "Buy me. Buy me, please." So he did.

His outfit reminded me of one of the most beautiful Sabbath days of my life. About a quarter of a century ago, when I was one of his students, he had asked me to join him and some members of his congregation who studied together on Sabbath afternoons at an estate overlooking Long Island Sound.

Our learning ended an hour or so before sunset and the departure of the Sabbath. He invited me to take a walk with him in the snow and the cold yellow light before the *havdalah* ceremony marking the end of the day. He was wearing a big fur coat that day, too, and he looked like a Polish Rebbe. We trudged through the driven snow and the vanishing sunlight. All I remember is his teaching presence and a kind of joke he made: "Here we are, Larry, crossing the frozen River Vistula."

Seeing him in front of the college in his fur coat brought it all back to me and I told him about the River Vistula. But he only smiled and, without missing a beat, said, "And the only reason I said it then was so that we could share this sweet memory now."

It occurs to me that we have here a new subcategory of déjà vu. It is not that we have the strange sensation of having been here before, but rather the even stranger sensation of, for at least a moment, understanding why we were where we were.

Lawrence Kushner, *Invisible Lines of Connection: Sacred Stories of the Ordinary* (Woodstock, VT: Jewish Lights Publishing, 1996), 132–33

CHAPTER FIVE

ה:א וַיְהִי בַּיּוֹם הַשְּׁלִישִׁי וַתִּלְבַּשׁ אֶסְתֵּר מַלְכוּת וַתַּעֲמֹד בַּחֲצַר בֵּית־
הַמֶּלֶךְ הַפְּנִימִית נֹכַח בֵּית הַמֶּלֶךְ וְהַמֶּלֶךְ יוֹשֵׁב עַל־כִּסֵּא מַלְכוּתוֹ
בְּבֵית הַמַּלְכוּת נֹכַח פֶּתַח הַבָּיִת:

5:1 ESTHER PUT ON ROYAL APPAREL ON THE THIRD DAY
AND STOOD IN THE INNERMOST COURTYARD OF THE
PALACE OPPOSITE THE PLACE WHERE THE KING SAT ON
HIS ROYAL THRONE FACING THE ENTRANCE.

This verse describes the scene in which Esther follows through on her promise to
Mordecai and prepares to approach the king. Given the king's reaction to Esther's
appearance in the next verse, her dress was probably provocative in some way, but
there is no way to confirm its nature. For the *Targum*, the description is inadequate.
Thus, it adds the following to its translation: "On the third day of Passover, Esther put
on royal raiment, and then the Holy Spirit rested on her. She rose up and prayed in
the courtyard of the royal court that was built opposite the royal house. The king sat
on the royal throne and looked at the entrance to the house. Esther said [to God],
'Master of the universe, don't hand me over to the hands of this uncircumcised man
and don't do what wicked Haman wants to do and what he did with Vashti—that he
gave the order to kill Vashti so that Ahasuerus could marry his daughter.' For that
reason, Haman had had all the young women brought to Hegai, his daughter among
them. By heavenly fiat, Haman's daughter was defiled by the contents of a chamber
pot, and her breath became really offensive. In haste, she was removed from the
group and married off to another man. [Esther continued her prayer.] 'May I find
mercy in Ahasuerus's eyes and may he not kill me. May he do what I ask and what
I will ask. And may You, O God, in Your great mercy, have compassion on Your
people and not hand over the children of Jacob to the hand of Haman, son of

Hammedatha, son of Ada, son of Biznai, son of Aphlitus, son of Diosos, son of Peros, son of Hamdan, son of Talyon, son of Athenisomus, son of Harum, son of Harsus, son of Shegar, son of Negar, son of Parmashta, son of Vayzatah, son of Agag, son of Sumkar, son of Amalek, son of Eliphaz, son of wicked Esau.'''

ה:ב וַיְהִי כִרְאוֹת הַמֶּלֶךְ אֶת־אֶסְתֵּר הַמַּלְכָּה עֹמֶדֶת בֶּחָצֵר נָשְׂאָה חֵן בְּעֵינָיו וַיּוֹשֶׁט הַמֶּלֶךְ לְאֶסְתֵּר אֶת־שַׁרְבִיט הַזָּהָב אֲשֶׁר בְּיָדוֹ וַתִּקְרַב אֶסְתֵּר וַתִּגַּע בְּרֹאשׁ הַשַּׁרְבִיט:

5:2 NO SOONER DID THE KING SEE ESTHER THE QUEEN STANDING IN THE COURTYARD THAN SHE WON HIS HEART. HE HELD OUT THE GOLDEN SCEPTER IN HIS HAND TO HER. ESTHER CAME CLOSE AND TOUCHED ITS TIP.

This verse exudes sexual innuendo. The *Targum* explains that Esther won over the heart of the king quickly when he saw her eyes filled with tears and her face turned heavenward.

ה:ג וַיֹּאמֶר לָהּ הַמֶּלֶךְ מַה־לָּךְ אֶסְתֵּר הַמַּלְכָּה וּמַה־בַּקָּשָׁתֵךְ עַד־חֲצִי הַמַּלְכוּת וְיִנָּתֵן לָךְ:

5:3 HE SAID TO HER, "QUEEN ESTHER, WHAT'S WRONG? WHAT DO YOU WANT? IF YOU WANTED HALF THE KINGDOM, IT WOULD BE YOURS."

Esther has the king where she wants him. He is clearly smitten with her. Yet, the *Targum* seems to limit the king's generous offer in its translation. For the *Targum*, the king adds, "except to rebuild the Temple that stands in the middle of my kingdom, because I have taken an oath to Geshem the Arabian, Sanballat the Horonite, and Tobiah the servant, the Ammonite [an allusion to Nehemiah 2:19] not to permit its being rebuilt. I fear that Jews may rebel against me if I do not do what you ask. Anything else that you ask for, I will do. It will be done with dispatch, and whatever else you wish will be given to you."

Rashi also understands "half the kingdom" as "in the middle of my kingdom," meaning the Land of Israel. He thinks that it refers to the rebuilding of the Temple that had begun in the time of Cyrus. However, according to Rashi, Cyrus changed his mind and stopped the work. Ahasuerus, who succeeded him on the throne, also prevented any rebuilding. Rashi does note that a literal understanding of the verse could be "If you ask me for half my kingdom, I will give it to you."

ה:ד וַתֹּאמֶר אֶסְתֵּר אִם־עַל־הַמֶּלֶךְ טוֹב יָבוֹא הַמֶּלֶךְ וְהָמָן הַיּוֹם אֶל־הַמִּשְׁתֶּה אֲשֶׁר־עָשִׂיתִי לוֹ:

5:4 ESTHER ANSWERED, "IF IT PLEASE THE KING, LET THE KING AND HAMAN COME TODAY FOR A FEAST THAT I HAVE PREPARED."

While readers, especially those who are familiar with the story, might understand the cleverness of the queen's request, the request comes as a bit of a surprise to Ahasuerus. Rashi notes (in the Babylonian Talmud, *M'gillah* 15b) that Esther's invitation to Haman might suggest to the king that Esther was attracted to Haman, causing Ahasuerus to become so jealous of Haman that he'd kill him. Rashi also explains that the word *mishteh* is used for "feast" because it comes from the word "to drink" and the feast is devoted to the drinking of wine.

ה:ה וַיֹּאמֶר הַמֶּלֶךְ מַהֲרוּ אֶת־הָמָן לַעֲשׂוֹת אֶת־דְּבַר אֶסְתֵּר וַיָּבֹא הַמֶּלֶךְ וְהָמָן אֶל־הַמִּשְׁתֶּה אֲשֶׁר־עָשְׂתָה אֶסְתֵּר:

5:5 THE KING SAID, "TELL HAMAN TO COME QUICKLY TO DO WHAT ESTHER WANTS." SO THE KING AND HAMAN CAME TO THE FEAST THAT ESTHER HAD PREPARED.

Esther's plan begins to unfold. "To do what Esther wants" is our idiomatic translation of the literal *laasot et d'var Esther*, "to do the word of Esther." The *Targum* expands the phrase as *l'me'bad yat pitgam g'zeirat Esteir*, "to do the word of the command of Esther," in order to emphasize how Esther has the king under her control.

81

ה:ו וַיֹּאמֶר הַמֶּלֶךְ לְאֶסְתֵּר בְּמִשְׁתֵּה הַיַּיִן מַה־שְּׁאֵלָתֵךְ וְיִנָּתֵן לָךְ וּמַה־בַּקָּשָׁתֵךְ עַד־חֲצִי הַמַּלְכוּת וְתֵעָשׂ׃

5:6 AT THE WINE FEAST, THE KING SAID TO ESTHER, "WHATEVER YOU ASK FOR WILL BE GIVEN TO YOU AND WHATEVER YOU WANT, EVEN UP TO HALF MY KINGDOM, IS YOURS."

The king's interest is piqued. While he could command Esther, he would rather respond to her wishes so that she might respond to his. This is part of the game of seduction that the couple is playing and the author is emphasizing. As it did in verse 3, the *Targum* limits the king's offer in its translation. According to the *Targum*, Esther can have everything she wants except the rebuilding of the Temple. Then the *Targum* repeats the king's reasoning here. Perhaps the *Targum* wants to minimize the possibility that its readers may understand the king to be a sympathetic character.

ה:ז וַתַּעַן אֶסְתֵּר וַתֹּאמַר שְׁאֵלָתִי וּבַקָּשָׁתִי׃

5:7 ESTHER REPLIED, "THIS IS WHAT I WANT AND THIS IS WHAT I ASK.

Rather than allow these words to function as an introductory statement, the *Targum* adds the following explanation: "I don't want half the kingdom, and I don't want the rebuilding of the Temple."

ה:ח אִם־מָצָאתִי חֵן בְּעֵינֵי הַמֶּלֶךְ וְאִם־עַל־הַמֶּלֶךְ טוֹב לָתֵת אֶת־
שְׁאֵלָתִי וְלַעֲשׂוֹת אֶת־בַּקָּשָׁתִי יָבוֹא הַמֶּלֶךְ וְהָמָן אֶל־הַמִּשְׁתֶּה
אֲשֶׁר אֶעֱשֶׂה לָהֶם וּמָחָר אֶעֱשֶׂה כִּדְבַר הַמֶּלֶךְ:

5:8 "O KING, IF YOU WILL DO ME THIS FAVOR AND BE WILLING TO GIVE ME WHAT I WANT AND DO WHAT I ASK, THEN COME, YOU AND HAMAN, TO ANOTHER FEAST THAT I AM ARRANGING FOR TOMORROW, AND THEN, O KING, I WILL DO WHAT YOU WANT."

While the king thinks that Esther is just being a responsive "harem girl" trying to please her king, Esther is instead offering herself—presumably sexually—in return for the saving of the Jewish people—a request that she has yet to make of the king. Again we see Esther using her sexuality, one of the few means available to women in the ancient world to assert any power.

In its translation, the *Targum* renders the phrase *kidvar hamelech* as *k'fitgam gezeirat malka*, "like the word of the commandment of the king." This emphasizes the importance of Esther's request.

Rashi explains that Esther's reference to "tomorrow" signifies her promise to fulfill the king's long-standing desire that she reveal to him her people and her birthplace. This seems to be more of Rashi's interest than is evidenced in the text. Commentators like Rashi cannot fathom the possibility that Esther operates in the palace without the intention of revealing her identity as a Jew when the circumstances require it of her. For Ibn Ezra, "tomorrow" suggests that Esther now sees a divine sign in the rise in Mordecai's status, a sign that she had waited for but not seen, even after having fasted.

In all likelihood, the two feasts are only to extend the tension in the text: When will Esther and her people be saved?

ה:ט וַיֵּצֵא הָמָן בַּיּוֹם הַהוּא שָׂמֵחַ וְטוֹב לֵב וְכִרְאוֹת הָמָן אֶת־מָרְדֳּכַי בְּשַׁעַר הַמֶּלֶךְ וְלֹא־קָם וְלֹא־זָע מִמֶּנּוּ וַיִּמָּלֵא הָמָן עַל־מָרְדֳּכַי חֵמָה:

5:9 Haman went out that day happy as could be, but when he saw Mordecai at the palace gate, who neither rose for him nor showed any fear of him, he became filled with rage at Mordecai.

Although Koehler-Baumgartner (p. 267) translates the word *za* as "tremble," we choose to translate it as "showed any fear," since it is Mordecai's lack of emotion that is paramount to the narrative. The author of the Book of Esther wants to emphasize that Haman becomes enraged because Mordecai totally ignores him.

The *Targum* elaborates and describes the extent of Haman's anger. Haman's rage is intensified when he sees Mordecai "and the children who were studying the words of the Torah in the Sanhedrin that Queen Esther had set up in the palace gate. [Moreover] Mordecai did not rise or tremble before Haman's idol; rather, he stuck out his right foot and showed him the bill of sale that it had been sold to him in exchange for a loaf of bread, which had been written on the legging of his pants leg." While the *Targum*'s additional comment is unusual and somewhat unclear, what is clear is that it is trying to point out that Mordecai refused to bow to Haman's idol and ridiculed Haman for his possession of something so powerless and banal.

ה:י וַיִּתְאַפַּק הָמָן וַיָּבוֹא אֶל־בֵּיתוֹ וַיִּשְׁלַח וַיָּבֵא אֶת־אֹהֲבָיו וְאֶת־זֶרֶשׁ אִשְׁתּוֹ:

5:10 Haman, however, controlled himself and went home. He sent for his friends and for Zeresh, his wife.

It is surprising that Haman controls his anger, since the previous verse indicates that he was filled with rage. The delay allows the suspense to mount, keeping the reader aware that Haman must be up to no good. In this verse, the entrance of Haman's wife into the conspiracy against the Jews of ancient Persia is foreshadowed (see 5:14). The *Targum* identifies her as ''the wicked Zeresh, daughter of Titni the governor of 'over the river.'''

While Rashi explains Haman's self-control as a fear of taking revenge without permission (of the king), Ibn Ezra suggests that the control is merely a means of waiting to reveal his secret plan until he reaches home. In relating *vayitapak* (controlled himself) to *l'hitapeik* in Genesis 45:1, where Joseph controls himself before revealing himself to his brothers, Ibn Ezra senses that the word means ''to endure.''

ה:יא וַיְסַפֵּר לָהֶם הָמָן אֶת־כְּבוֹד עָשְׁרוֹ וְרֹב בָּנָיו וְאֵת כָּל־אֲשֶׁר גִּדְּלוֹ הַמֶּלֶךְ וְאֵת אֲשֶׁר נִשְּׂאוֹ עַל־הַשָּׂרִים וְעַבְדֵי הַמֶּלֶךְ:

5:11 HAMAN TOLD THEM [HIS FRIENDS] ABOUT HIS GREAT WEALTH, HIS MANY SONS, AND HOW THE KING HAD HONORED HIM BY PROMOTING HIM ABOVE ALL THE MINISTERS AND OFFICIALS OF THE KING.

Perhaps Haman's way to deal with his anger is to boast of his accomplishments and status to his friends. The *Targum* expands what Haman tells those whom he has assembled as his audience. Haman goes on to describe his recent increase in power. He explains that he has been appointed one of the dukes of the king and that the strongest of his sons, 208 in number, are part of his entourage, not counting ten others who are generals commanding districts, and not counting those sons who serve as royal scribes. Haman tells his audience that the king has promoted him and has appointed him to supervise all the nobles and king's servants.

Readers may find it odd that Haman would gather his friends and wife to tell them about the number of his sons and the extent of his wealth. Ibn Ezra suggests that Haman is making the point that his sons and his wealth pale in comparison to his promotion by the king and to the honor of being invited to have supper with the queen—which we learn in the next verse.

ה:יב וַיֹּאמֶר הָמָן אַף לֹא־הֵבִיאָה אֶסְתֵּר הַמַּלְכָּה עִם־הַמֶּלֶךְ אֶל־
הַמִּשְׁתֶּה אֲשֶׁר־עָשָׂתָה כִּי אִם־אוֹתִי וְגַם־לְמָחָר אֲנִי קָרוּא־לָהּ
עִם־הַמֶּלֶךְ:

5:12 HAMAN WENT ON TO SAY, "ONLY ME, BESIDE THE
KING, DID THE QUEEN BRING TO THE FEAST THAT SHE
HAD PREPARED. TOMORROW I AM ALSO INVITED WITH
THE KING."

This verse provides further explication of the previous verse. It clarifies how privileged
Haman feels—and how surprised he will be when he realizes that he has misread
what is happening.

ה:יג וְכָל־זֶה אֵינֶנּוּ שֹׁוֶה לִי בְּכָל־עֵת אֲשֶׁר אֲנִי רֹאֶה אֶת־מָרְדֳּכַי
הַיְּהוּדִי יוֹשֵׁב בְּשַׁעַר הַמֶּלֶךְ:

5:13 "BUT WHAT GOOD IS IT TO ME WHEN I KEEP SEEING
THAT JEW MORDECAI SITTING IN THE PALACE GATE?"

Haman will not allow himself to luxuriate in his apparent good fortune. This verse
reveals how intensely Haman hates Mordecai, a hatred he extends to the entire
Jewish people. The *Targum* adds that Mordecai sat "in the Sanhedrin with his young
men [that is, disciples]." The scene described by the *Targum* would certainly infuriate
Haman even more. Knowing that Haman does not seem to enjoy the honor afforded
him, Rashi looks for a reason from Jewish textual tradition to explain it. He cites a text
from the Babylonian Talmud (*M'gillah* 15a) in which the Sages say that Mordecai
showed Haman the bill of sale that proved that Haman had been forced to sell
himself as a slave because of his failure to provide the required provisions for the
armies over which he and Mordecai had been appointed.

ה:יד וַתֹּאמֶר לוֹ זֶרֶשׁ אִשְׁתּוֹ וְכָל־אֹהֲבָיו יַעֲשׂוּ־עֵץ גָּבֹהַּ חֲמִשִּׁים אַמָּה
וּבַבֹּקֶר אֱמֹר לַמֶּלֶךְ וְיִתְלוּ אֶת־מָרְדֳּכַי עָלָיו וּבֹא־עִם־הַמֶּלֶךְ אֶל־
הַמִּשְׁתֶּה שָׂמֵחַ וַיִּיטַב הַדָּבָר לִפְנֵי הָמָן וַיַּעַשׂ הָעֵץ:

5:14 HIS WIFE ZERESH AND HIS FRIENDS SAID TO HIM, "BUILD A GALLOWS FIFTY CUBITS HIGH. TELL THE KING TO HAVE MORDECAI HANGED ON IT, AND THEN YOU CAN BE HAPPY WHEN YOU GO TO THE FEAST." HAMAN THOUGHT IT WAS A GREAT IDEA. SO HE HAD THE GALLOWS BUILT.

In this verse, the plan to kill Mordecai seems to come from others, although Haman quickly champions the idea. In its translation, the *Targum* explicates Zeresh's suggestion and displays the extent to which the *Targum* is often as much midrash as it is translation and commentary:

Zeresh his wife and all of his friends said to him, "If we may, let us say something to you, what can we do to Mordecai the Jew, if he is one of the righteous who are created in the world? [Then they list a variety of occasions in which individuals in the Bible placed in life-threatening situations have been saved by God.] We can't kill him with a sword, for such a sword has been turned against us. If we mean to cast a stone at him, David had already cast a stone at Goliath the Philistine. If we throw a brazen serpent [near him], he had already split it and escaped from it. [This is a reference to II Chronicles 33:11, where the word *n'chushtayim*, 'fetters of bronze,' according to Koehler-Baumgartner (p. 691), is taken to refer to a bronze ox into which Manasseh was put for execution (see also Jastrow, p. 1694).] Were we to throw him into the Great Sea, the Israelites already split the sea and crossed through it. [See Exodus 14:15ff.] Were we to throw him into a blazing fire, from such a fire Hananiah, Mishael, and Azariah had already escaped. [See Daniel 3:19ff.] Were we to throw him into a lion's den, [we know that] the lions did not harm Daniel. [See Daniel 6:17ff.] If we were to throw him to the dogs [to be eaten], the mouths of dogs, for the sake of the Israelites, were stopped up in the land of Egypt. [See Exodus 11:7.] Were we to exile him to the wilderness, they [the Israelites] have increased and become stronger. In what way can we kill him? What kind of death can we impose on him? Were we to imprison him, it was from the prison that Joseph was taken to be brought to high estate. Were we to take a knife to his throat, such a knife was already taken from the throat of Isaac. Were we to blind him and leave him alone, he will kill us as Samson [killed his enemies].

"We don't know what other kind of punishment that humans might suffer could be applied to him. So a large gallows should be set up at the gate of his house. Let his blood be poured out. Let his body be raised on the gallows and let all the Jews and all his associates and all his friends see him." Heaven and earth together heard about the gallows that Haman had prepared for Mordecai.

Haman waited anxiously until morning. As soon as it did [morning came], he entered into the presence of the king and asked him about the gallows. Haman had not sent someone else nor had he slept until he went and brought the carpenters and the forgers of arms and the smiths so that they could make knives. The sons of Haman rejoiced, and Zeresh his wife played on a harp along with wicked Haman. He said, "I will give a reward to the carpenters and smiths who work on the gallows that I have arranged." At the moment that Haman the wicked went to erect the gallows, a divine voice came from the highest heaven saying, "Well done, wicked Haman. It is good for you O son of Hammedatha. It is good that from Haman came the word to make the gallows for himself."

From the day that Esther had invited him for service, the Israelites were afflicted and they would say to each other, "Because of this man we are hated. Each and every day Esther has beseeched the king that we kill him and she has invited him to her service." At that moment, the House of Jacob poured out their hearts and trusted their Parent in heaven, saying, "Answer us and deliver us from this, as a servant turns his eye to his master and as the maidservant turns her eye to her mistress, thus do we turn our eyes to You until the time when You will reveal Yourself and deliver us from those who hate us and who are our opponents who revile us. Thus God will hear your prayer and do what you ask. It will happen at night because God delivers you from our enemies at night, as God did in delivering you from Pharaoh and from Sennacherib, who rose against you."

Geshem, Sanballat, and Tobiah (Tuviah)

Mentioned in Nehemiah 2:10, Sanballat held a position of authority in Samaria when Nehemiah went up to Jerusalem to rebuild its ruined walls. He vainly attempted to hinder this work (Nehemiah 2:10, 2:19, 4:1–12, 6:1–16). His daughter became the wife of one of the sons of Joiada, a son of the High Priest, much to the chagrin of Nehemiah (13:28).

Tobiah (or Tuviah) joined with those who opposed the rebuilding of Jerusalem after the Babylonian exile (Nehemiah 2:10). He was a man of great influence, which he exerted in opposition to the Jews, and "sent letters" to Nehemiah "to put him in fear" (Nehemiah 6:17–19).

Geshem was probably chief of the Arabs south of ancient Israel, one of the enemies of the Jewish people after the return from the Babylonian exile (Nehemiah 2:19, 6:1–2). He joined Sanballat and Tuviah in their opposition to rebuilding the walls of Jerusalem.

GLEANINGS

Purim—Story of Intermarriage Gone Right?

It sounds like an everyday story: A beautiful young Jewish woman marries a rich and powerful non-Jewish man.

She's raised in an acculturated upper-class household, where the *religion* of power and influence is of greater importance than the religion of her ancestors. Synagogue attendance and Jewish education are not priorities.

So when our heroine meets a non-Jew who can give her everything she wants and more, they marry. Eventually she comes to identify with her people and, luckily for all of us, her husband also throws in his lot with the Jews at a crucial moment in history.

The Purim narrative is rarely seen through the prism of a successful interfaith marriage, yet clearly the holiday we celebrate is based on the relationship between a Jewish woman and a non-Jewish man.

Esther married Ahashuerus, the king of Persia. Because of her *beauty*, she was chosen to become queen—or, more accurately, Harem Girl No. 1.

Like the other adult-themed components of the story, the various marital aspects of Purim are swept under the rug to create a kinder, gentler holiday we can share with our children.

Ignored are the thinly veiled sexual innuendoes, the horrendous slaughter of Haman's relatives and any difficult questions about an intermarriage gone right.

Instead, we are left with Queen Esther beauty pageants for young girls—which some may say perpetuate the objectification of women—and synagogue youth carnivals that really have little to do with Purim.

Throughout the ages, rabbis have avoided the difficult questions, instead making apologies for Esther's behavior.

In classic Jewish literature, commentators say Esther intentionally hid her Jewish identity until she was able to come out of the closet in front of her husband.

Some claim that the events never even occurred. Others say that use of her Persian name, Esther (rather than her Hebrew name, Hadassah) proves that the girl was complicit in Mordechai's complex plan for Jewish survival.

There are even those who've figured out how Esther supposedly was fastidious about keeping kosher while living in the palace and taking part in the king's parties!

None is willing to admit that were it not for an interfaith marriage that worked, the Jews of ancient Persia might all have been destroyed.

Perhaps the rabbis are afraid that such an admission would amount to implied acquiescence with those who choose to intermarry today—as if an ancient historical precedent affects the decisions individuals make about love, life, and Jewish continuity in today's secular society.

The Purim story is timeless. That is its strength.

But this timelessness is not a result of a lachrymose approach to Jewish history, in which we see enemies rise up against us time and again, regardless of where we live.

Rather, it is Esther's relationship to Ahashuerus that catapults the story through the portals of Jewish history.

Esther and Mordechai were heroes, but so was Ahashuerus [even if it were for the wrong reason, that is, to save his wife because he was insulted]. The Purim story shows that in the face of Jewish destruction—whether it comes from the outside, as in ancient Persia, or from inside the American Jewish community—intermarriage has the potential to help us rather than destroy us, if we are willing to bring the intermarried into our Jewish family and invite them to cast their lot with our own.

Kerry Olitzky, "Purim—The Story of an Intermarriage Gone Right?"
Washington Jewish Week, March 1, 2001, 17

Lessons about Power

Purim may be a wacky, crazy holiday filled with silliness, costumes, and the farcical shpiel, but buried in its story are significant and serious lessons about power. Within the story of Esther you can detect a certain attitude toward power. It is true that the

Purim story of Esther does find moments to tell its jokes about power and authority, too: The supposedly supreme king is generally clueless, all the important decisions are made by the eunuchs, the book's heroine is a woman..., and in the end, the Jews get the last laugh by turning the tables on Haman, whose ancestors are the arch-enemies the Amalekites. You could say that for our people the book of Esther has functioned as a humorous release from the grim reality of living at the whim of our hosts in Persia (or, name-your-own-location, depending on whichever host culture we Jews found ourselves through the centuries)....

We American Jews are like Esther—in the palace of the king. Perhaps we have attained our royal position for just a time like this. In a time when we see injustices committed within our society, across the oceans, and yet within our reach, we should remember Mordecai's words to Esther. Our window to influence decision-makers may be limited. Our relationships are key. And who knows, maybe we have come to this moment in human history at just this time to bring about justice and fairness, having been given a unique opportunity to do so.

Andrew Vogel, Temple Sinai Bulletin (Brookline, MA), March 2006

Why Fast?

I. Restraint: We are to say no to food. If we can succeed in this regard, we strengthen the control necessary to refrain from the more serious act of grabbing someone or something not ours....

II. Humility: Fasting not only teaches restraint, but when one does not eat, he or she becomes less haughty. An individual who fasts is not so arrogant or high and mighty and thus, hopefully, better able to acknowledge shortcomings. Alas, in our society the "I" is too swollen; many of us are very self-righteous and personally over-bearing because of some apparent success. A distant relative, rather anti-cerebral, gives "learned" treatises and regards himself a self-styled theologian simply because he has "arrived" materially....

III. Empathy: Fasting not only involves the ability to say "no" to temptation and to be less self-righteous; it also better allows us to experience the hunger, pain, or pathos of those who are hurting all year long.

Frederick Schwartz, Teacher of Torah, ed. Elliott Lefkovitz
(Chicago: Temple Sholom, 1997), 74, 75

Wrestling with Gender Politics

My experience of Purim as an opportunity for boundary-crossing transgression is nothing new; in fact it's a very old tradition. The oldest surviving text of Yiddish Purim parody-plays (called Purimspiels) is a manuscript from 1697 known as the "Achashverosh-spiel," a play considered so vulgar at the time that it was burned by the government of Frankfort, Germany. In 1728, the government of Hamburg banned the performance of Purimspiels entirely. Today, Purimspiels are common in yeshiva and religious communities. But the celebrations have also been reclaimed in recent years by... progressives of all types, in part because of the possible feminist readings of the theater to create powerful spectacles and performances that critique, amplify, and challenge the politics of our times, the Jewish community, and the Megillah's story itself. . . .

With the between-the-lines vision of Purim's transgressive potential, we can ask real and deep questions. Is Esther a brave heroine or a subordinating woman spinning back and forth between the demands of various men in her life, making good for herself by capitalizing on the betrayal of other, stronger women? Is Mordechai a brave Jewish hero, or a patronizing and arrogant man who would gladly do to another people what he wished not done to his own? He won't bow to a king, but he tells Esther to bow to her husband, the king. Is Haman truly evil, or was his history written by the victors who killed his whole people and needed to vilify him to justify a brutal "regime change"? Is Vashti the . . . [non-Jewish] heroine of this story? Is the King really a fool, or, as many commentators suggest, the worst of all—a lecherous old man with access to endless virgins, eager to sign off on any genocide that doesn't affect his property or his status? We have to wonder why those eunuchs were plotting to kill him, and look who starts and ends with real power!

Modern Purim celebrations use the traditional play as a vehicle for popular education around a broad range of issues by playing with the iconic roles typified by the Megilla's characters: good girl, bad girl, stupid king, valiant citizen, evil politician. These traditional players can easily and informatively be mixed up with any combination of modern kings, s/heroes, insider/outsider activists, popular resistance movements and evildoers-ex-machina. . . .

For those of us who don't fit the mainstream Jewish community norms, Purim has become an opportunity to come out of the corners and challenge our own community by manifesting our fabulous otherness. . . . On Purim those of us who, like Pesach's wicked child, don't tow those party lines, exhibit our politics . . . without fear of rejection and repression. (Or so we hope.)

The stage directions for the 2004 Immigrant Justice Purim Spiel offer some modern midrash that may allow us to harness the power of Purim to challenge fundamentalism in years to come:

> Hadassah stresses that on Purim, if you are confused, you are doing the right thing. [She] knows there are many paths towards holy disorder, many routes to the mystical place of misunderstanding. . . . The more we don't understand, the more dyslexic we feel, the more we are entering into the practice of Purim, the more we will be supercharged, renewed, transformed.
>
> Emily Nepon, "Wrestling with Esther: Purim Spiels, Gender, and Political Dissidence," *Zeek Magazine*, March 2006, http://www.zeek.net/603/Purim/

CHAPTER SIX

וֹ:א בַּלַּיְלָה הַהוּא נָדְדָה שְׁנַת הַמֶּלֶךְ וַיֹּאמֶר לְהָבִיא אֶת־סֵפֶר
הַזִּכְרֹנוֹת דִּבְרֵי הַיָּמִים וַיִּהְיוּ נִקְרָאִים לִפְנֵי הַמֶּלֶךְ:

6:1 THAT NIGHT, THE KING COULD NOT SLEEP, SO HE
ORDERED THE BOOK OF RECORDS, THE BOOK CON-
TAINING THE EVENTS OF EVERY DAY, TO BE BROUGHT.
AND IT WAS READ BEFORE HIM.

While the words *sefer hazichronot* (book of records) and *divrei hayamim* (literally,
"words of the days," which we have as "the book containing the events of every
day") seem to be redundant, our translation attempts to make sense of both terms by
noting that the records contained in the book were of daily events. In recognition of
the reality of the times, the author assumes that the king was illiterate and could not
read the record book himself.

In its extensive commentary on this verse, the *Targum* expands on the word that
begins the verse, "night." This is as much a continuation of the *Targum*'s explanation
of the previous verse as it is an explanation of this verse. It also retells the story once
again. In its translation, the *Targum* begins by listing many acts of redemption that
occur at night, as a way of promising the reader that they too will be redeemed from
whatever they are currently encountering. The *Targum* anticipates the consequences
of what will be shared in the next verse by embellishing its commentary once again.
While the next verse reveals the plot of Bigthan and Teresh, Mordecai is assured that
the plot will be spoiled and the Jewish community will be saved—a foreshadowing of
the eventual saving of the Jewish community from Haman, as well.

Rashi thinks that the king's inability to sleep is actually a miracle (see Babylonian
Talmud, *M'gillah* 19a). He also thinks that the reading aloud of the book of records
was a common practice for kings who suffered from insomnia. He adds that the
Rabbis believed Ahasuerus was convinced that Haman and Esther had plotted evil

94

against him. Perhaps, thought Ahasuerus, there is someone who knows their plans and will reveal them to me if I do them a favor. So he had the book of records brought to him so that he could see whom he owed a favor.

Ibn Ezra prefers the view of the *Targum* and understands "the king" as the Divine Sovereign. Accordingly he quotes Psalms 121:4, "The Guardian of Israel neither slumbers nor sleeps." Ibn Ezra notes that some think that the bringing of the book of records was simply to amuse Ahasuerus by hearing what happened in the past. Nevertheless, Ibn Ezra agrees with the view of others who suggest that the king had the book brought forward because he was distressed by the feeling that he had not fulfilled a vow that he had made.

ו:ב וַיִּמָּצֵא כָתוּב אֲשֶׁר הִגִּיד מָרְדֳּכַי עַל־בִּגְתָנָא וָתֶרֶשׁ שְׁנֵי סָרִיסֵי הַמֶּלֶךְ מִשֹּׁמְרֵי הַסַּף אֲשֶׁר בִּקְשׁוּ לִשְׁלֹחַ יָד בַּמֶּלֶךְ אֲחַשְׁוֵרוֹשׁ:

6:2 It was recorded there [in the book of records] that Mordecai had reported that Bigthan and Teresh, two of the royal eunuchs, guardians of the portal, were plotting to kill Ahasuerus.

In its translation, the *Targum* clarifies the report, taking *sarisei hamelech* (royal eunuchs) to mean "royal officers" and *shomrei hasaf* (guardians of the portal) to mean "guardians of the palace." The *Targum* also tells us where the plotted assassination was to take place, by adding the words "in the bedchamber," *b'veit d'macheih*.

ו:ג וַיֹּאמֶר הַמֶּלֶךְ מַה־נַּעֲשָׂה יְקָר וּגְדוּלָה לְמָרְדֳּכַי עַל־זֶה וַיֹּאמְרוּ נַעֲרֵי הַמֶּלֶךְ מְשָׁרְתָיו לֹא־נַעֲשָׂה עִמּוֹ דָּבָר:

6:3 "What honor or privilege has been conferred upon Mordecai for all this?" asked the king. "Nothing at all has been done for him," asserted the king's attendants.

The author describes the events of the story as if they are coincidental. It just so happens that the king can't sleep. It just so happens that he asks that his chronicles be read to him. Nevertheless, the irony of the next verse is clear: the presence of Haman in the courtyard of the palace will initiate the salvation of the Jewish people in ancient Persia. The process begins with the saving of Mordecai.

וּ:ד וַיֹּאמֶר הַמֶּלֶךְ מִי בֶחָצֵר וְהָמָן בָּא לַחֲצַר בֵּית־הַמֶּלֶךְ הַחִיצוֹנָה
לֵאמֹר לַמֶּלֶךְ לִתְלוֹת אֶת־מָרְדֳּכַי עַל־הָעֵץ אֲשֶׁר־הֵכִין לוֹ:

6:4 "Who is in the courtyard?" the king asked. Haman had just entered the outer courtyard of the palace to ask the king to hang Mordecai on the gallows that he had prepared for him.

Once again, the *Targum* fills in what it perceives as missing information from the story. The one whom "the king asked," the *Targum* explains, was "a man standing in the courtyard." It uses the infinitive form *l'mitzlav*, which may mean either "to hang" or "to impale." In doing so, it does not specify the vehicle to be used to execute Mordecai, but it could be either by impalement or by hanging.

וּ:ה וַיֹּאמְרוּ נַעֲרֵי הַמֶּלֶךְ אֵלָיו הִנֵּה הָמָן עֹמֵד בֶּחָצֵר וַיֹּאמֶר הַמֶּלֶךְ
יָבוֹא:

6:5 The king's servants said to him, "Haman is standing out in the courtyard." The king replied, "Let him come in."

This verse simply helps the reader to understand how Haman ends up in the king's presence.

ו:ו וַיָּבוֹא הָמָן וַיֹּאמֶר לוֹ הַמֶּלֶךְ מַה־לַעֲשׂוֹת בָּאִישׁ אֲשֶׁר הַמֶּלֶךְ חָפֵץ בִּיקָרוֹ וַיֹּאמֶר הָמָן בְּלִבּוֹ לְמִי יַחְפֹּץ הַמֶּלֶךְ לַעֲשׂוֹת יְקָר יוֹתֵר מִמֶּנִּי:

6:6 Haman entered and the king said to him, "What should be done for a person whom the king wishes to honor?" Haman thought to himself, "Who could that be more than me?"

As might be expected, Haman thinks that the king wants to bestow an honor on him. He is so self-centered that he can't imagine anything else to be possible.

Ibn Ezra teaches an important spiritual lesson in his comment to this verse. He says, "God alone knows the secrets of the heart." Thus, for Ibn Ezra, the phrase "Haman thought to himself" is ironic if it is used to prove that the Book of Esther was the product of prophecy. Haman thought his intentions were hidden, but because the Book of Esther is the product of prophecy (and by extension, God's knowledge), it is ironic that Haman believes he can hide the truth. Ibn Ezra notes that others think the phrase might be a reasonable conclusion that is based on Haman's subsequent activity or that Haman himself might have told somebody later. As proof that the Book of Esther was given by the Holy Spirit, Ibn Ezra gives the example of the parallel Torah statement that Esau "spoke to himself" (Genesis 27:41).

ו:ז וַיֹּאמֶר הָמָן אֶל־הַמֶּלֶךְ אִישׁ אֲשֶׁר הַמֶּלֶךְ חָפֵץ בִּיקָרוֹ:
ו:ח יָבִיאוּ לְבוּשׁ מַלְכוּת אֲשֶׁר לָבַשׁ־בּוֹ הַמֶּלֶךְ וְסוּס אֲשֶׁר רָכַב עָלָיו הַמֶּלֶךְ וַאֲשֶׁר נִתַּן כֶּתֶר מַלְכוּת בְּרֹאשׁוֹ:

6:7 Haman answered the king, "For that person whom the king wishes to honor,

6:8 "Let a royal robe be brought that the king himself has worn, along with a horse with a royal crest on its head that the king himself has ridden.

The reader knows that when Haman makes this suggestion, he thinks that the king has him in mind. These symbols of royalty will be authenticated by others having seen them initially worn by the king. Haman assumes that once the symbols are associated with him, he will then be accorded the same respect as the king.

The *Targum* expands Haman's request by designating the color of the robe he wants to wear as purple, as well as telling the reader that the king first put it on when he first assumed his royal status. The *Targum* also tells the reader why Haman wants the particular horse he chooses: it is the horse that the king rode on the day he became king. While it might seem that Haman is interested merely in the royal garments, he really is interested in taking over Ahasuerus's position as king.

Ibn Ezra explains that the royal servants will bring the robe and the horse. He notes that some think that Haman really wants the crown that the king wears but decides not to provoke the king. So he settles for the royal crest on the head of the horse.

ו:ט וְנָתוֹן הַלְּבוּשׁ וְהַסּוּס עַל־יַד־אִישׁ מִשָּׂרֵי הַמֶּלֶךְ הַפַּרְתְּמִים וְהִלְבִּישׁוּ אֶת־הָאִישׁ אֲשֶׁר הַמֶּלֶךְ חָפֵץ בִּיקָרוֹ וְהִרְכִּיבֻהוּ עַל־הַסּוּס בִּרְחוֹב הָעִיר וְקָרְאוּ לְפָנָיו כָּכָה יֵעָשֶׂה לָאִישׁ אֲשֶׁר הַמֶּלֶךְ חָפֵץ בִּיקָרוֹ:

6:9 "Let the royal robe and the horse be presented by one of the king's aristocratic princes. Let them put the robe on the person whom the king wants to honor, and let them lead him riding on the royal horse through the city streets. Then let them proclaim before him: 'This is what is done for the one whom the king wants to honor.'"

Haman wants everyone to see him being led through the streets of the city by its nobles. Employing the common literary technique of using loan words to add local color, the author uses the word *part'mim* (aristocratic, nobles). The word has already been used in 1:3.

The *Targum* translates *part'mim* as *istartigin* (chiefs of camps) and tells the readers that the *turb'yanei* (young nobles) are the ones who would dress the individual to be honored. The word *istartigin* comes from Greek through Latin and gives us the English word "strategic."

Rashi explains that the royal crest mentioned in the previous verse is excluded in this verse because the king was not happy about the suggestion of someone else (besides his horse, of course) wearing his crest. Ibn Ezra reminds readers that no servant of the king was even permitted to ride on the king's horse, implying that the entire scenario that Haman proposes is preposterous.

וּ:י וַיֹּאמֶר הַמֶּלֶךְ לְהָמָן מַהֵר קַח אֶת־הַלְּבוּשׁ וְאֶת־הַסּוּס כַּאֲשֶׁר
דִּבַּרְתָּ וַעֲשֵׂה־כֵן לְמָרְדֳּכַי הַיְּהוּדִי הַיּוֹשֵׁב בְּשַׁעַר הַמֶּלֶךְ אַל־תַּפֵּל
דָּבָר מִכֹּל אֲשֶׁר דִּבַּרְתָּ:

6:10 THE KING SAID TO HAMAN, "HURRY UP. GET THE ROBE AND THE HORSE AS YOU HAVE SAID. AND DO THIS FOR MORDECAI THE JEW WHO SITS IN THE ROYAL GATE. LEAVE NOTHING OUT OF WHAT YOU HAVE SAID."

While the reader knows that this is about to happen, Haman is shocked to hear the king's words. The *Targum* sees this verse as a kind of dialogue initiated by Haman to delay matters: "The king says, 'Do this for Mordecai.' Haman answers, 'Which Mordecai?' Says the king, 'Mordecai the Jew.' Haman responds, 'There are many Jews in Shushan named Mordecai.' To that the king says, 'The Mordecai for whom Esther arranged a Sanhedrin in the royal gate.' Haman then says, 'I would rather that you kill me than to command me to do this thing.' The king finally says, 'Hurry up and do it and leave nothing out.'"

וּ:יא וַיִּקַּח הָמָן אֶת־הַלְּבוּשׁ וְאֶת־הַסּוּס וַיַּלְבֵּשׁ אֶת־מָרְדֳּכָי וַיַּרְכִּיבֵהוּ
בִּרְחוֹב הָעִיר וַיִּקְרָא לְפָנָיו כָּכָה יֵעָשֶׂה לָאִישׁ אֲשֶׁר הַמֶּלֶךְ חָפֵץ
בִּיקָרוֹ:

6:11 SO HAMAN TOOK THE ROBE AND DRESSED MORDECAI
IN IT AND [PLACED HIM ON] THE HORSE AND LED HIM
RIDING ON IT THROUGH THE STREETS OF THE CITY,
CALLING OUT BEFORE HIM, "THIS IS WHAT IS DONE
FOR THE ONE WHOM THE KING WANTS TO HONOR."

This is a rather ironic scene. Haman is forced to honor the very person whom he
wishes to kill. Again, the *Targum* explains that the robe is purple, which designates the
royalty of its wearer.

וּ:יב וַיָּשָׁב מָרְדֳּכַי אֶל־שַׁעַר הַמֶּלֶךְ וְהָמָן נִדְחַף אֶל־בֵּיתוֹ אָבֵל וַחֲפוּי
רֹאשׁ:

6:12 MORDECAI THEN RETURNED TO THE ROYAL GATE,
WHILE HAMAN HURRIED HOME, MOURNING AND
GRIEVING.

Haman is not a happy man. The phrase *chafui rosh*, literally "with a covered head,"
seems to have the idiomatic meaning of "grieving." It may also anticipate *uf'nei
Haman chafu* of Esther 7:8, when Haman's face is covered on his way to being
hanged.

The *Targum* is not satisfied with the description of events in the written story and
offers its own perspective on what took place: "Mordecai returned to the Sanhedrin
at the royal gate, took off the purple royal robe, put on sackcloth and sat upon ashes,
and began praying until evening. Agitated, Haman hurried to his home, mourning for
his daughter and wrapping his head like a mourner for his daughter and his disgrace."
According to a tradition that is preserved in the *Targum* on 5:1, Haman had hoped
that his daughter would marry the king and become queen. For that reason, he had

advised the execution of Vashti. Now all that Haman had hoped for has crumbled before him. Esther is queen. Mordecai is honored. And Haman has become the instrument of such an honor.

Both the *Targum* and Rashi note that Mordecai's return to the gate and to mourners' clothing emphasizes his humility and altruism. Even thus honored, he is concerned about the "impending destruction of his people," according to Rashi.

ו:יג וַיְסַפֵּר הָמָן לְזֶרֶשׁ אִשְׁתּוֹ וּלְכָל־אֹהֲבָיו אֵת כָּל־אֲשֶׁר קָרָהוּ וַיֹּאמְרוּ לוֹ חֲכָמָיו וְזֶרֶשׁ אִשְׁתּוֹ אִם מִזֶּרַע הַיְּהוּדִים מָרְדֳּכַי אֲשֶׁר הַחִלּוֹתָ לִנְפֹּל לְפָנָיו לֹא־תוּכַל לוֹ כִּי־נָפוֹל תִּפּוֹל לְפָנָיו:

6:13 Haman told his wife Zeresh and all of his friends everything that had happened to him. His advisors and his wife said to him, "If Mordecai, before whom you are beginning to fall, is of Jewish descent, you can't win against him. You will surely be brought down."

This verse may come as a surprise to most readers. One would expect Haman's friends and his spouse to be supportive and comforting. Contained in the words of the verse is a warning to all who might try to bring down the Jewish people. They might also be saying to him, "You'd better do something soon if you are to beat him."

We render the phrase *zera ha-Y'hudim*, literally "the seed of the Jews," as "Jewish descent." The *Targum* translates the term more universally as *mizera d'tzadikaya*, "from the seed of the righteous."

Rashi is more poetic in his comment. He thinks that Zeresh tells Haman that the Jewish people are compared to the stars, an allusion to Genesis 22:17. When stars are in the ascendant, the Jewish people rise up even to the heavens. When the stars descend, the Jewish people go down. She is apparently suggesting that Haman is misreading the stars (perhaps even a reference to the *purim*). The Jewish people is in a period of ascent, not descent.

The text seems to say that it is Haman's advisors rather than his friends who predict that evil will befall him. Yet Ibn Ezra uses this verse as an opportunity to offer practical advice about friends, grouping Haman's friends and advisors together. When calamity comes, says Ibn Ezra, even one's friends don't predict a good outcome.

וּיד עוֹדָם מְדַבְּרִים עִמּוֹ וְסָרִיסֵי הַמֶּלֶךְ הִגִּיעוּ וַיַּבְהִלוּ לְהָבִיא אֶת־
הָמָן אֶל־הַמִּשְׁתֶּה אֲשֶׁר־עָשְׂתָה אֶסְתֵּר:

6:14 WHILE THEY WERE STILL TALKING TO HIM, THE ROYAL EUNUCHS CAME AND RUSHED HAMAN AWAY TO THE FEAST THAT ESTHER HAD PREPARED.

Because of his focus on Mordecai (and his own self-aggrandizement), Haman has forgotten about the party to which Esther had invited him.

GLEANINGS

The Sacred Art of Fasting

A distinctive feature of Judaism is its philosophy of integrating the spiritual with the physical. Jews do not reject the physical in favor of the spiritual; rather, they recognize the opportunity that living a physical existence provides for the exercise and strengthening of the spiritual. In this world, the physical and the spiritual are inextricably intertwined, and we must use both to activate our ultimate growth and to achieve our raison d'être....

Fasting is difficult, but it is the very fact of its difficulty that gives us the opportunity to connect to God in a stronger way. The sublimation of our own desires to eat in favor of the directive to fast is itself an offering. In addition, harnessing the emptiness that fasting engenders to bring about a deeper level of repentance, along with the sacrifice that we can "offer" to God, makes fasting a precious opportunity for connecting ourselves with God's will.

> Aliza Bulow, in *The Sacred Art of Fasting* by Thomas Ryan
> (Woodstock, VT: Jewish Lights Publishing, 2005), 26, 28

A Kavanah/Meditation for Purim

Purim is a celebration of the human potential for transformation. It is a holiday that recognizes a people's ability to overturn despair and put joy in its place, to move from mourning to feasting....

The reading of the *Megillah* and the meal are moments of celebratory bliss: we cloak ourselves in brilliant disguises and masquerade through the synagogue. We drink *ad d'lo yada*—until we can no longer distinguish between Mordecai and Haman, thereby removing all distinctions, rejecting discernment. The objective of *Purim* is for each of us to have, even momentarily, the recognition that we are all at once both Mordecai and Haman—each of us has the potential for both greatness and wickedness....

All of the customs associated with Purim—the drinking, the singing, the partying, and the gift giving—are, at their essence, about recognizing the innate ability of every person to transform him- or herself or situation, to move from sorrow to gladness.

This *Purim* may we celebrate the unlimited human potential innate to each of us.

Congregation B'nai Jeshurun (New York City)

Men Are from Baghdad and Women Are from Damascus

One of the hidden messages of the Purim story, as told in the book of Esther, is about the Torah and its positive attitude toward women (rumors to the contrary notwithstanding). . . .

Just look at the contrast between the conventional, non-Jewish attitude towards women at that time, and the way that Mordechai and Esther worked together in perfect husband-wife dynamic. Whereas the Persians were busy partying and attempting to denigrate their women by parading them around in an immodest fashion (which seems to have been the standard, accepted mode of behavior at that time), the Jewish people, as represented by Mordechai and Esther, were far more progressive in their male-female relationships. They understood full well that Men are from Baghdad and Women are from Damascus. Mordechai could only suggest a possible plan to save the Jews, but it was up to Esther, with her insight and intuition, to ultimately formulate that plan in a way that would bring it to a successful conclusion. What a team! What mutual self-respect and understanding between husband and wife!

David Zauderer, Torah from Dixie, 2001, http://tfdixie.com

The Message of Jewish Unity

The Purim story reminds us that we are all in this together. All of us play a part in the future of the Jewish people no matter how connected we may be right now.

As Haman develops his plot to kill all of the Jews, it is Mordechai who reminds his niece, Queen Esther that she too will be killed by Haman unless she uses her access to power to stop him. Yes, she is the Queen. Yes, she is a Jew that is not so involved in her Judaism anymore, but it does not matter. She is still a Jew. And if she does not do anything to stop Haman, she too will become a victim.

So in the end, Esther becomes a Heroine, because she takes bold and courageous steps to save her people. At first, she fears approaching the King. But Mordechai tells her that perhaps it was for just such a crisis that she was granted a royal position. Thus fortified, she speaks to the king and saves her people. Yes, Esther becomes a hero. Yes, her access to power saves our people. In the end she stands up for her people . . . by risking her life to identify as a Jew. . . .

Purim is a reminder to us that we need to leave the door open for those who have left to return because we may never know when we may need them and they may need us. . . .

Haman wanted to destroy all the Jews, young and old, secular and religious together. In order to achieve his goal, Haman told King Ahasuerus that the opportune time had arrived because, "There is a certain people scattered and separate among the peoples throughout all the provinces of your kingdom" (Esther 3:8). The Midrash comments that Haman recognized that this was the perfect time to attack the Jews because we weren't simply "scattered and separate." Rather, we were divided and contentious. We were fighting with each other, and disunity reigned. Haman knew that when Jews do not get along with each other, their enemy has the ability to defeat them.

Our rabbis comment that, for this reason, Esther instructed Mordechai, "Go assemble all the Jews who are present in Shushan" (4:16). Esther didn't say to Mordechai, "Go and assemble only these 'types' of Jews." Rather, she clearly instructed that "all Jews," no matter their age, background, or what their observance level might be, must pray together. If we wish to survive, Esther knew, we must be united! . . .

I believe that this is the reason that the rabbis predicted that Purim would be observed even in the messianic days, when almost all other Jewish holidays would be abolished (*Midrash Mishlei* 9). By continuing to observe Purim in the Messianic Age as we do now, Jews will have a constant reminder of the importance of Jewish unity that this holiday represents.

Brian Strauss, Purim Sermon, Congregation Beth Yeshurun
(Houston, TX), Purim 2006

Esther Images

... The story of Purim is one in which Queen Esther is posited as a heroine, a woman of valor, a mighty image of feminine courage that has endured through the ages. That's why little girls dress up as Esther on Purim each year in and year out. Still, it strikes me that even Esther's heroism—brought about, though it was, by earning the title of Miss Persian Empire—was damped as a woman's achievement by the villainy of Vashti that seems to necessarily accompany it. ...

In a recent essay, the poet Katha Pollitt wrote about the implicit sexism of the popular animated feature *The Little Mermaid*, and worried about the effects that movie would have on her young daughter. Entire seminars have been held to reexamine all sorts of prejudices in the works of the Brothers Grimm. And these are just *fairy tales*. But Judaism is a living religion, practiced on some level even by Jews who claim to be atheists. For many people, the Bible is a living document, a record of the word of God, a blueprint for life much like the American Constitution. The story of Purim is taught to children not as a cute bit of folklore but as a piece of history, as nothing less than the truth. And in the case of Vashti, the problem is not even with the Bible itself—it's with the way it is being taught. While religious people are, justifiably, wary of any suggestions to change the text itself to make it more modern and readable—and less sexist—they could hardly object to altering the way it is taught so that Vashti can be seen as brave—or at the very least, not evil—in her defiance of the king. After all, how are girls going to grow up to be strong, self-determined women when one of the first things they learn is that if you get pimples and refuse to pose nude in public, you deserve to get killed? What kind of message is that?

Elizabeth Wurtzel, Essay, 1998

CHAPTER SEVEN

ז:א וַיָּבֹא הַמֶּלֶךְ וְהָמָן לִשְׁתּוֹת עִם־אֶסְתֵּר הַמַּלְכָּה:

7:1 SO THE KING AND HAMAN CAME TO FEAST WITH
ESTHER, THE QUEEN.

While the verse uses the word *lishtot* (to drink), we think that the sense of the verse
requires a more idiomatic "to feast" or, in more colloquial language, "to party."

ז:ב וַיֹּאמֶר הַמֶּלֶךְ לְאֶסְתֵּר גַּם בַּיּוֹם הַשֵּׁנִי בְּמִשְׁתֵּה הַיַּיִן מַה־שְּׁאֵלָתֵךְ
אֶסְתֵּר הַמַּלְכָּה וְתִנָּתֵן לָךְ וּמַה־בַּקָּשָׁתֵךְ עַד־חֲצִי הַמַּלְכוּת
וְתֵעָשׂ:

7:2 ON THE SECOND DAY OF THE WINE FEAST, THE KING
AGAIN ASKED ESTHER, "WHAT DO YOU WISH, O
ESTHER MY QUEEN? IT WILL BE GIVEN TO YOU! WHAT
DO YOU WANT? EVEN IF IT IS HALF MY KINGDOM, IT
IS YOURS."

The text reminds us that the king is smitten by Esther. She is now in the position to ask
of him whatever she wants.

ז:ג וַתַּעַן אֶסְתֵּר הַמַּלְכָּה וַתֹּאמַר אִם־מָצָאתִי חֵן בְּעֵינֶיךָ הַמֶּלֶךְ וְאִם־
עַל־הַמֶּלֶךְ טוֹב תִּנָּתֶן־לִי נַפְשִׁי בִּשְׁאֵלָתִי וְעַמִּי בְּבַקָּשָׁתִי:

7:3 ESTHER THE QUEEN ANSWERED, "YOUR MAJESTY, IF
I HAVE FOUND FAVOR IN YOUR EYES AND IF IT PLEASES
THE KING, FOR MY WISH, FOR MY REQUEST, GIVE ME
AND MY PEOPLE LIFE.

As part of Esther's plan to convince the king to spare the lives of the Jews, and in recognition of her delicate position as a Jewish queen, she continues to be obsequious. Nevertheless, her request comes as a shock to the king.

The *Targum* emphasizes Esther's humble piety and adds "Esther raised her eyes to heaven" to the beginning of its translation of this verse. It adds further drama to her request. The *Targum* depicts Esther as saying, "Save my life from the hands of the enemy, and deliver my people from the hand of the opponent for my request."

Because Esther's plea is somewhat cryptic—how can the king possibly know what she is referring to?—Rashi explains that the first part of Esther's wish is that she not be killed on the thirteenth of Adar, the date on which the death of her people has been ordered. She then asks the king to deliver the Jewish people, for "what interest could the king have in their destruction?"

Ibn Ezra has a much more straightforward understanding of the text. He contends that Esther is simply asking the king to save her life.

ז:ד כִּי נִמְכַּרְנוּ אֲנִי וְעַמִּי לְהַשְׁמִיד לַהֲרוֹג וּלְאַבֵּד וְאִלּוּ לַעֲבָדִים
וְלִשְׁפָחוֹת נִמְכַּרְנוּ הֶחֱרַשְׁתִּי כִּי אֵין הַצָּר שֹׁוֶה בְּנֵזֶק הַמֶּלֶךְ:

7:4 "FOR MY PEOPLE AND I HAVE BEEN SOLD TO BE
DESTROYED, TO BE KILLED, TO BE WIPED OUT. WERE
WE ONLY TO BE SOLD AS MALE OR FEMALE SLAVES,
I WOULD HAVE KEPT SILENT, FOR OUR PROBLEM IS NOT
WORTH TROUBLING THE KING."

In order to get the verse to make sense idiomatically, certain adjustments are made in the translation of this verse. Although the word *tzar* is translated by Koehler-

Baumgarten (p. 1502) as "anxiety," that translation does not quite fit the sense of the verse, so we translate it as "problem." The Kittel Bible (p. 1250, note on 7:4), a scholarly text that takes into consideration various extant manuscripts, proposes *hatzalah shoveh*. The translation of the last clause would be "the deliverance [*hatzalah*] is not worth the king's trouble."

Since the issue of being sold as slaves has not come up previously, Rashi explains that Esther says that were the king to have the Jews sold as slaves and he to receive the sale price, or even were he to keep them as his personal slaves, she would have kept quiet. That would not have been enough to trouble him with a request.

זה:ה וַיֹּאמֶר הַמֶּלֶךְ אֲחַשְׁוֵרוֹשׁ וַיֹּאמֶר לְאֶסְתֵּר הַמַּלְכָּה מִי הוּא זֶה וְאֵי־זֶה הוּא אֲשֶׁר־מְלָאוֹ לִבּוֹ לַעֲשׂוֹת כֵּן:

7:5 King Ahasuerus then asked Queen Esther, "Who is he? What man is he who dares do such a thing?"

The reader can hear the anger rising in the king's voice. In order to emphasize the king's anger, the *Targum* adds these words: "From where does this impudent, guilty, and rebellious man whose heart has moved him to do this come?"

The text twice uses the phrase *vayomer* ("he said," which we translate as "asked"), a Hebrew literary device that is not evident in the English translation. Rashi, however, believes that this doubling requires explanation. He claims that the first use of "he said" suggests that the king communicated with the queen by messenger and the second time he spoke to her directly.

Ibn Ezra, on the other hand, thinks that the repetition of "he said" indicates that the king became instantly incensed and so furious that he repeated himself. The continuation of the phrase in Hebrew, *mi hu zeh v'ei zeh hu*, literally "Who is he and what is he?" which we have rendered as "Who is he? What man is he who...?" is taken by Ibn Ezra as a further indication of the king's fury.

וַתֹּאמֶר אֶסְתֵּר אִישׁ צַר וְאוֹיֵב הָמָן הָרָע הַזֶּה וְהָמָן נִבְעַת מִלִּפְנֵי הַמֶּלֶךְ וְהַמַּלְכָּה: ז:ו

7:6 ESTHER ANSWERED, "IT IS WICKED HAMAN WHO IS THE VICIOUS FOE." HAMAN WAS SEIZED BY TERROR BEFORE THE KING AND QUEEN.

Haman is shocked to hear what Esther has to say. Esther describes Haman with two synonyms, *tzar v'oyeiv* (foe and enemy). We take it to mean "vicious foe." The *Targum* uses the opportunity to list Esther's charges against Haman in its translation of the verse: "He planned that night to kill the king in his bedroom. He intended that day to put on the royal vestments. He wished to ride the royal steed. He wanted to put the gold crown on his head." In sum, he wished to rebel against the king and usurp the kingdom. The *Targum* adds that word came from heaven at the same moment as Esther's revelation to the king to provide glory to the righteous Mordecai, who was brother to Aba ben Yair and who was the last of a long line of people stretching back to Abraham.

וְהַמֶּלֶךְ קָם בַּחֲמָתוֹ מִמִּשְׁתֵּה הַיַּיִן אֶל־גִּנַּת הַבִּיתָן וְהָמָן עָמַד לְבַקֵּשׁ עַל־נַפְשׁוֹ מֵאֶסְתֵּר הַמַּלְכָּה כִּי רָאָה כִּי־כָלְתָה אֵלָיו הָרָעָה מֵאֵת הַמֶּלֶךְ: ז:ז

7:7 FURIOUS, THE KING GOT UP FROM THE WINE FEAST AND WENT TO THE PALACE GARDEN. HAMAN REMAINED TO PLEAD FOR HIS LIFE FROM ESTHER THE QUEEN, SENSING THAT THE KING HAD ALREADY DECIDED HIS FATE.

Seeing the way the king has left, Haman realizes he is doomed. Left alone with Esther, he pleads for his life. The reader is left to wonder why the king left. Perhaps he left the room in order to retch, sickened by what he just heard. Or maybe he left to maintain his composure in front of his court or because he simply couldn't stand the sight of Haman. In the *Targum's* embellished translation, the king raises his eyes and sees angels who resemble the ten sons of Haman cutting down trees in the garden. For that reason, the king arises from the wine feast to see what is happening. Haman then gets up to plead for his life, sensing that the king has decided that he (Haman) is evil. It is important to note that the *Targum's* comment describes the king's concern for the destruction of trees, not for the destruction of human beings. This is the same king who partied with his drunken friends and banished his wife. He also willingly agreed to Haman's plan before he knew that Esther would be killed as a result. The *Targum* is not prepared to forget his former actions so readily.

Rashi understands the verse a little differently. He explains that *chaltah* (concluded), which we translate as "already decided," is a reference to the "evil, hatred, and revenge that were now finished," that is, Haman's evil power and life are now coming to an end.

ז:ח וְהַמֶּלֶךְ שָׁב מִגִּנַּת הַבִּיתָן אֶל־בֵּית מִשְׁתֵּה הַיַּיִן וְהָמָן נֹפֵל עַל־
הַמִּטָּה אֲשֶׁר אֶסְתֵּר עָלֶיהָ וַיֹּאמֶר הַמֶּלֶךְ הֲגַם לִכְבּוֹשׁ אֶת־
הַמַּלְכָּה עִמִּי בַּבָּיִת הַדָּבָר יָצָא מִפִּי הַמֶּלֶךְ וּפְנֵי הָמָן חָפוּ:

7:8 At the very moment that the king returned from the palace garden to the wine feast room, Haman fell down on Esther's couch. The king exploded, "Does he mean to rape the queen even though I am here in the palace?" The king gave the order, and they covered Haman's face.

What bothers the king is not what happens to the Jewish people or even what happens to the queen. Rather, he is enraged by what he perceives as *lese majesty*, a personal affront to him as king. How dare Haman pay no regard to the king's status?

The *Targum* wants to fill in the gaps in the story. After all, if the king left the room in the previous verse, how is he back in the room in this verse? So the *Targum* has him return in fury from the palace garden to the wine feast room. There he sees Haman sprawled on Esther's couch. What the king did not see, according to the *Targum*, was that Haman was pushed by the angel Gabriel, something with which Rashi agrees. The king concludes, "Truly Haman's only purpose to come here was to lie with the queen, even though I was in the palace." He takes counsel with all

111

the various peoples, language groups, and nations in his empire to decide what to do with Haman. The king gives the order, and as a symbol of disgrace, they cover Haman's face.

Ibn Ezra sees the episode more literally. He explains that Haman is pleading with Esther, prostrating himself at Esther's feet. And he falls when he sees (*k'reotah*, literally "when she saw") the king reenter the room.

ט:ז וַיֹּאמֶר חַרְבוֹנָה אֶחָד מִן־הַסָּרִיסִים לִפְנֵי הַמֶּלֶךְ גַּם הִנֵּה־הָעֵץ אֲשֶׁר־עָשָׂה הָמָן לְמָרְדֳּכַי אֲשֶׁר דִּבֶּר־טוֹב עַל־הַמֶּלֶךְ עֹמֵד בְּבֵית הָמָן גָּבֹהַּ חֲמִשִּׁים אַמָּה וַיֹּאמֶר הַמֶּלֶךְ תְּלֻהוּ עָלָיו:

7:9 THEN HARBONAH, ONE OF THE ROYAL EUNUCHS, SAID, "THERE IS A GALLOWS, FIFTY CUBITS HIGH, AT HAMAN'S HOUSE. HAMAN HAD IT BUILT FOR MORDECAI, THE ONE WHOSE REPORT SAVED THE KING." "HANG HIM ON IT!" THE KING ORDERED.

Haman receives what he was planning for Mordecai. While the *Targum* changes these eunuchs (*hasarisim*) into *rabanaya* (courtiers), it adds to its translation "whose report had saved the king from being killed [*isht'zeiv mi-ktol*]."

In his commentary on this verse, Rashi explains another one of Haman's sins. Perhaps feeling that the gallows is too severe a punishment for *attempted* murder, he notes, "Haman did something else wrong. He prepared a gallows to hang a friend of the king who had saved the king from poison." Taking the life of a person who had saved the king was a crime deserving of capital punishment.

For Ibn Ezra, the king's order is a direct result of the appearance of Elijah the Prophet in the form of a eunuch. This is according to a legend that Ibn Ezra quotes. Legends about Elijah, who is to herald the coming of the Messiah, abound in Jewish literature and claim that he can be hiding as anyone—usually the lowliest of individuals in society. This is why we must treat everyone with equanimity and dignity.

ז:י וַיִּתְלוּ אֶת־הָמָן עַל־הָעֵץ אֲשֶׁר־הֵכִין לְמָרְדֳּכָי וַחֲמַת הַמֶּלֶךְ
שָׁכָכָה:

7:10 So they hanged Haman on the gallows that he
had built for Mordecai. Then the king's anger
subsided.

Haman is executed on the instrument of death that he had constructed for
Mordecai's demise. While this seems like a straightforward verse, one reading of the
text suggests that Haman's death is not in the service of justice but only meant to
dissipate the king's anger—a reading that presents a difficult ethical construct. Yet
none of the classical commentators choose to comment on this verse.

Aba ben Yair

Aba ben Yair is Mordecai's brother. (Their father was mentioned in Esther 2:5.) The
Targum makes an attempt to identify him in Isaiah by understanding the word "mighty
one" as an abbreviated proper name: "Thus says the Sovereign, the God of heaven's
hosts, the Mighty One [*avir*] of Israel: 'Ah, I will ease Me of My adversaries, and avenge
Me of My enemies'" (Isaiah 1:24); "And I will feed those who oppress you with their
own flesh; and they will be drunken with their own blood, as with sweet wine; and all
flesh shall know that I the Eternal am your Savior and your Redeemer, the Mighty One
[*avir*] of Jacob" (Isaiah 49:26); "You will also suck the milk of the nations, and will suck
the breast of kings; and you will know that I the Eternal am your Savior, and I, the
Mighty One [*avir*] of Jacob, your Redeemer" (Isaiah 60:16).

GLEANINGS

Esther You Know Everything

You know everything
Put eloquent speech in my mouth,
Before this lion to change this man.
I hate this man,
He is fighting You.
So there must be an end to him and those who support him, he is evil.
Save me by Your hand and help me.
I, who stand alone.
I have no one but You.

Your slave has not eaten at his table,
nor have I honored his feast,
nor drunk the wine of his libations.
Two faces I wear,
The mask of the Queen
And the Jew filled with fear.
Your slave has had no joy
from the day I was brought here,
Except in You.

Elizabeth Swados, *Bible Women*
(New York: Swados Enterprises, 1995)

The Reconciliation of Adulthood and Childhood

Rav Joseph Soleveitchik, the revered leader of modern orthodoxy for many decades, held that Esther embodies two divergent aspects of the human soul. On the one hand, Esther is a master of cunning. Mordecai's initial plan was for Esther to run to the king and tell him all of Haman's wicked plans and plead for the nation (4:8) but Esther demurs. She immediately intuits that diplomacy and guile are called for. She plans the banquets and "sets up" Haman's demise. It is an act of cunning par excellence. And cunning, according to Rav Soleveitchik, is the act of adults. Only maturity allows one to understand human nature in such a way as to devise a plan such as this.

But Esther is also the exemplar of prayer and fasting. Esther commands all Israel to fast for her (4:16). Esther thus becomes the model of communal prayers in times of peril. But while cunning, Soloveitchik says, is a quintessential adult quality, prayer is an activity which children excel in. "An adult is too realistic, too cynical, too hardened by life. To truly pray you must believe the unbelievable and hope for the impossible. True prayer is also that which swells up either from total despair or total ecstasy. The adult moderates his emotions and doesn't allow himself to 'let loose' and go to the extreme of feeling. But a child gives free rein to the feelings of anger, happiness, disappointment and joy."

Jews, Soloveitchik contends, are asked to be adult and child simultaneously. They must act as messengers of God with maturity and cunning, but they must also be able to pray, to find the deep wells of emotion within them and let that spill over to God. Esther symbolizes this ability to be both cunning and prayerful, adult and child simultaneously. For Soloveitchik, Esther's ability to synthesize cunning and prayer lay in her femaleness. Women are both more mature and more emotionally deep than men. I would with respect disagree with the Rav's gender views, but uphold his profound sense of Esther as child and adult. Jews are asked by our tradition to be both adult and child. We are asked to be open to wonder as a child is, but also cognizant of life's difficulties and pains in a way that a child is not.

Daniel Judson, "Esther: The Reconciliation of Adulthood and Childhood"
(Temple Beth David, Canton, MA, 2007)

The Monica Metaphor

In France, they called me Monica—and boy, was that the joke that wouldn't quit. They chuckled "Monica" when I walked down the street, winked "Monica" when I picked up a baguette, sniggered "Monica" when I bought a bottle of wine at the corner store. This was back in 1998, the post-college year I spent loafing in Paris, and here's the weird part: At first, I didn't even know what they were talking about. My name was, and is, Lauren. . . .

Jewess. I suppose it's not inherently offensive—I mean, it's certainly better than a hundred other derogatory names you could call a Jew. But still it rankles. The word "Jewess" brings to mind heavy locks of thick black hair, long skirts, clinking bracelets, a musky odor. Something closer to a gypsy dancer than a rabbi's wife, except with the belly covered and without the castanets. A Jewess sounds juicy and slightly dirty, like a lot of other words that end in –ess—mistress, seductress, stewardess. And Jewish women, as far as I can tell, are the only females of a particular religious group to be designated with that voluptuous suffix. You never hear of the Mormoness, the Presbyterianess, the Buddhess. But there she is, the Jewess: exotic and exoticized, heavy-breasted and smoky-voiced. Never mind that most of the Jewish women I know are wildly overworked, too stressed-out to find the time to be seductive. Never mind that in their current pop-culture depictions, Jewish women tend to be emasculating shopaholics—Jewish American Princesses bearing Daddy's AmEx, not shaking tambourines. And never mind that, as far as clinking bracelets go—that ain't the Monica I remember, and it is sure . . . isn't me.

Lauren Grodstein, "The Monica Metaphor," in *The Modern Jewish Girl's Guide to Guilt*, ed. Ruth Andrew Ellenson (New York: Plume, 2006), 163–72

Esther's Beauty

Esther was beautiful by the conventions of her culture. She knew that being thought beautiful was a blessing. It made her feel good about herself, and it drew people to her, making her feel success and accomplishment for having done nothing at all. She was also aware that people found her beautiful for reasons that had little to do with her appearance. She could access the beauty of the other and radiate it back. It was this conviction—that beauty was a two-way matter—that gave Esther the courage to find her way into the palace of Shushan and the heart of the king. . . .

Consider trying out Esther's beauty ritual. It's simple enough. Begin by turning away from the mirror after you have completed getting ready for the day in whatever way makes you feel good about yourself. Then, think about the people whom you plan to encounter in the course of the day. Imagine them and recall what it is about them that you admire. Think of specific details: the inner peace and grace of your yoga instructor; the ability of a coworker to make puns; your brother-in-law's sense of responsibility. Then repeat Esther's chant: "I look into your eyes. You think I am beautiful, but it is because you are beautiful to me. In this circle, we become precious to one another." When you see these people whose special gifts you've imagined, do not be surprised to discover that they can see their best selves reflected in your eyes.

Vanessa L. Ochs, Sarah Laughed: Modern Lessons from the
Wisdom and Stories of Biblical Women (New York: McGraw-Hill, 2005), 64, 66

CHAPTER EIGHT

ח:א בַּיּוֹם הַהוּא נָתַן הַמֶּלֶךְ אֲחַשְׁוֵרוֹשׁ לְאֶסְתֵּר הַמַּלְכָּה אֶת־בֵּית הָמָן צֹרֵר הַיְּהוּדִים וּמָרְדֳּכַי בָּא לִפְנֵי הַמֶּלֶךְ כִּי־הִגִּידָה אֶסְתֵּר מַה הוּא־לָהּ:

8:1 THAT DAY KING AHASUERUS GAVE ESTHER THE QUEEN ALL OF THE PROPERTY OF HAMAN, THE ENEMY OF THE JEWS. MORDECAI CAME INTO THE KING'S PRESENCE, FOR ESTHER HAD INFORMED HIM HOW MORDECAI WAS RELATED TO HER.

While Esther does not ask for Haman's property, the king gives it to her in any case. A literal translation of the Hebrew *beit Haman* (house of Haman) may suggest limiting the gift to only his house. Yet the *Targum* suggests that all of Haman's possessions were transferred to Esther: *enashei beiteih, v'yat kol tisb'roy, v'yat kol otreih*, ''people of his household, his entire treasure house, and all of his wealth.''

This verse does not specify how Mordecai is related to Esther. But Ibn Ezra explains that Mordecai is Esther's uncle.

ח:ב וַיָּסַר הַמֶּלֶךְ אֶת־טַבַּעְתּוֹ אֲשֶׁר הֶעֱבִיר מֵהָמָן וַיִּתְּנָהּ לְמָרְדֳּכַי וַתָּשֶׂם אֶסְתֵּר אֶת־מָרְדֳּכַי עַל־בֵּית הָמָן:

8:2 HE [THE KING] NOW GAVE TO MORDECAI THE SIGNET RING THAT THE KING HAD TAKEN BACK FROM HAMAN. ESTHER THEN PLACED MORDECAI IN CHARGE OF HAMAN'S PROPERTY.

Although it might have been inferred by the reader from the king's actions as described in previous verses, the king takes back his signet ring—a symbol of royal

118

authority—from Haman. Esther then gives Haman's property to Mordecai. Mordecai now owns the property of the very person who sought to destroy him.

The *Targum* uses the word *situmta* (signet) to explain that *tabato* (literally, "his ring") was the king's "signet ring." It also specifies the extent of Mordecai's power: he was "in charge" (*rav v'sarchan*, literally "master and manager") of Haman's family.

Ibn Ezra wants the reader to realize how daunting a task the transfer of wealth from Haman to Mordecai is. He notes that *he-evir* ("transfer," which we translate as "gave") means the taking of something from one person that is then given to another. We know that the king was the only man wealthier than Haman. According to Ibn Ezra, Haman's vast fortune is attested to by his owning of many slaves, as well as extensive property. These all need to be transferred to Mordecai—a complex task indeed.

ח:ג וַתּוֹסֶף אֶסְתֵּר וַתְּדַבֵּר לִפְנֵי הַמֶּלֶךְ וַתִּפֹּל לִפְנֵי רַגְלָיו וַתֵּבְךְּ
וַתִּתְחַנֶּן־לוֹ לְהַעֲבִיר אֶת־רָעַת הָמָן הָאֲגָגִי וְאֵת מַחֲשַׁבְתּוֹ אֲשֶׁר
חָשַׁב עַל־הַיְּהוּדִים:

8:3 ESTHER SPOKE TO THE KING ONCE AGAIN, FALLING TO
HIS FEET AND WEEPING. SHE BEGGED HIM TO AVERT
THE EVIL: HAMAN THE AGAGITE'S PLOT AGAINST THE
JEWS.

While Ibn Ezra suggests that when Esther first approached the king it was to destroy Haman, and only this time does she ask him to save her people, this separation is not obvious from the verse. It is clear, however, that Esther continues to approach her role carefully. She does not assume that just because the king has executed Haman and given her his possessions (which she has transferred to Mordecai) that she can presumptuously approach the king. She again throws herself at the king's mercy, or more literally at his feet. Nevertheless, as is evidenced in the next verse, she has learned how to manipulate him and get her way.

ח:ד וַיּוֹשֶׁט הַמֶּלֶךְ לְאֶסְתֵּר אֵת שַׁרְבִט הַזָּהָב וַתָּקָם אֶסְתֵּר וַתַּעֲמֹד לִפְנֵי הַמֶּלֶךְ:

8:4 THE KING STRETCHED OUT HIS GOLDEN SCEPTER TO ESTHER, AND ESTHER GOT UP AND STOOD BEFORE HIM.

The sexual innuendo in this verse is clear.

ח:ה וַתֹּאמֶר אִם־עַל־הַמֶּלֶךְ טוֹב וְאִם־מָצָאתִי חֵן לְפָנָיו וְכָשֵׁר הַדָּבָר לִפְנֵי הַמֶּלֶךְ וְטוֹבָה אֲנִי בְּעֵינָיו יִכָּתֵב לְהָשִׁיב אֶת־הַסְּפָרִים מַחֲשֶׁבֶת הָמָן בֶּן־הַמְּדָתָא הָאֲגָגִי אֲשֶׁר כָּתַב לְאַבֵּד אֶת־הַיְּהוּדִים אֲשֶׁר בְּכָל־מְדִינוֹת הַמֶּלֶךְ:

8:5 SHE SAID, "IF IT PLEASE YOUR MAJESTY, IF YOU FAVOR ME, IF THE MATTER SEEMS PROPER TO YOU, AND IF I AM PLEASING TO YOU, LET AN ORDER BE SENT TO RECALL THE DISPATCHES THAT CONTAINED HAMAN SON OF HAMMEDATHA THE AGAGITE'S PLAN TO DESTROY THE JEWS IN ALL OF THE KING'S PROVINCES.

The intentionally obsequious nature of Esther's approach is made clear by the author. She grovels and employs a posture of humility to persuade the king. While the American idiom would suggest that Esther speaks to the king in the second person, our translation is in the royal third person. This indirect form of speech reflects the reality of his power and her lack of it. Esther can plead, but only the king can act.

ח:ו כִּי אֵיכָכָה אוּכַל וְרָאִיתִי בָּרָעָה אֲשֶׁר־יִמְצָא אֶת־עַמִּי וְאֵיכָכָה אוּכַל וְרָאִיתִי בְּאָבְדַן מוֹלַדְתִּי:

8:6 "HOW WILL I ENDURE SEEING THE DISASTER THAT WILL HAPPEN TO MY PEOPLE? HOW WILL I ENDURE SEEING THE DESTRUCTION OF MY FAMILY?"

Plaintively, Esther continues her plea to the king, making it clear that Haman's order would impact on her and her family even if her own life, as queen, could be spared.

ח:ז וַיֹּאמֶר הַמֶּלֶךְ אֲחַשְׁוֵרֹשׁ לְאֶסְתֵּר הַמַּלְכָּה וּלְמָרְדֳּכַי הַיְּהוּדִי הִנֵּה בֵית־הָמָן נָתַתִּי לְאֶסְתֵּר וְאֹתוֹ תָּלוּ עַל־הָעֵץ עַל אֲשֶׁר־שָׁלַח יָדוֹ בַּיְּהוּדִים:

8:7 THEN KING AHASUERUS SAID TO QUEEN ESTHER AND MORDECAI THE JEW, "BECAUSE HAMAN INTENDED TO ATTACK THE JEWS, I HAVE GIVEN HIS PROPERTY TO ESTHER AND HAVE HANGED HIM ON THE GALLOWS.

This verse reflects both the king's lack of understanding of the situation and also heightens the suspense of the narrative.

In the verse, *asher shalach yado* (literally, "stretched out his hand") idiomatically means "to attack." However, as presented, the proposed attack has not yet occurred. Hence, we translate the phrase as "intended to attack."

For Rashi, the king's words imply that all the people in his realm would realize that all things follow the royal will and that the king favors the Jewish people. Thus, all that the Jewish people might say should be believed, and there is no reason to recall the earlier dispatches. All that is needed is for the Jews of Persia to write any new dispatches that they feel necessary.

ח:ח וְאַתֶּם כִּתְבוּ עַל־הַיְּהוּדִים כַּטּוֹב בְּעֵינֵיכֶם בְּשֵׁם הַמֶּלֶךְ וְחִתְמוּ בְּטַבַּעַת הַמֶּלֶךְ כִּי־כְתָב אֲשֶׁר־נִכְתָּב בְּשֵׁם־הַמֶּלֶךְ וְנַחְתּוֹם בְּטַבַּעַת הַמֶּלֶךְ אֵין לְהָשִׁיב:

8:8 "WRITE WHATEVER YOU WANT ABOUT THE JEWS AND SEAL IT WITH THE KING'S SIGNET RING, FOR ANYTHING WRITTEN IN THE KING'S NAME AND SEALED WITH THE KING'S SIGNET RING CANNOT BE REVOKED."

In this statement, the Jewish community's problem emerges. Even though the king has implied that his former decree would not be followed, this verse seems to suggest that—because the dispatch had been sealed by the signet ring when it was in Haman's possession—the decree is still standing as an order of the king. Rashi explains that *ein l'hashiv*, "cannot be revoked," suggests that "it would not be fitting to revoke and so make the king's word false."

Ibn Ezra asks the obvious question, "Would it not be sufficient to send out [additional] dispatches to save the Jewish people? Why did he have to send out dispatches to them [the Jewish people, that gave them permission] to kill their enemies?" Ibn Ezra answers his own question. He suggests that Mordecai is very astute. He knows about the original dispatches and their effect. The king tells him that according to the laws of the Medes and the Persians, dispatches sealed with the royal signet cannot be recalled. Since Haman, second to the king, sent those dispatches sealed with the royal signet, they remain in force. The only way to deal with the effect of the dispatches is to kill those who received them, which is why Mordecai sends instructions to kill the enemies of the Jewish people.

ח:ט וַיִּקָּרְאוּ סֹפְרֵי־הַמֶּלֶךְ בָּעֵת־הַהִיא בַּחֹדֶשׁ הַשְּׁלִישִׁי הוּא־חֹדֶשׁ סִיוָן בִּשְׁלוֹשָׁה וְעֶשְׂרִים בּוֹ וַיִּכָּתֵב כְּכָל־אֲשֶׁר־צִוָּה מָרְדֳּכַי אֶל־הַיְּהוּדִים וְאֶל הָאֲחַשְׁדַּרְפְּנִים־וְהַפַּחוֹת וְשָׂרֵי הַמְּדִינוֹת אֲשֶׁר מֵהֹדּוּ וְעַד־כּוּשׁ שֶׁבַע וְעֶשְׂרִים וּמֵאָה מְדִינָה מְדִינָה וּמְדִינָה כִּכְתָבָהּ וְעַם וָעָם כִּלְשֹׁנוֹ וְאֶל־הַיְּהוּדִים כִּכְתָבָם וְכִלְשׁוֹנָם:

8:9 THE KING'S SCRIBES WERE SUMMONED AT THAT TIME, ON THE TWENTY–THIRD DAY OF THE THIRD MONTH, THAT IS, THE MONTH OF SIVAN. AT MORDECAI'S DIRECTION, ORDERS WERE SENT TO THE JEWS, TO THE SATRAPS, TO THE GOVERNORS, AND TO THE OFFICIALS OF THE 127 PROVINCES THAT EXTENDED FROM INDIA TO ETHIOPIA, TO EVERY PROVINCE IN ITS OWN SCRIPT, AND TO EACH PEOPLE IN ITS OWN LANGUAGE AND TO THE JEWS IN THEIR SCRIPT AND THEIR LANGUAGE.

At Mordecai's instigation, the king wants to make sure that this dispatch is disseminated throughout his kingdom and readily understood by everyone. That is why it is written in many different alphabets and languages. The *Targum*'s use of the Greek loanword *istartilosin* to render "governors" indicates the impact of the Greco-Roman world on the Jewish community of Palestine. In order to help the reader appreciate the breadth of the kingdom, Ibn Ezra tells us that "India" was the most western (literally, "left side") part of the kingdom.

ח:י וַיִּכְתֹּב בְּשֵׁם הַמֶּלֶךְ אֲחַשְׁוֵרֹשׁ וַיַּחְתֹּם בְּטַבַּעַת הַמֶּלֶךְ וַיִּשְׁלַח סְפָרִים בְּיַד הָרָצִים בַּסּוּסִים רֹכְבֵי הָרֶכֶשׁ הָאֲחַשְׁתְּרָנִים בְּנֵי הָרַמָּכִים:

8:10 In the name of King Ahasuerus, Mordecai wrote the orders and sealed them with the royal signet and sent them by couriers riding racing mares used as relay horses in the royal post.

Mordecai wants to make sure that the order that permits the Jewish people to defend themselves, to kill their enemies before they are killed, reaches the Jewish community quickly. Since he has the king's resources at his disposal, he employs the most efficient means to do so. Nevertheless, the last part of the verse presents challenges of translation. There are a number of technical terms for various kinds of horses. We follow Koehler-Baumgartner in the translation of these terms: *harechesh*, "relay horses" ("for the postal roads," p. 1238), *haachasht'ranim*, "royal horses" (p. 37), and *b'nei haramachim*, "racing mares" (p. 1244). Our translation attempts to provide an order and avoid any redundancy in the employment of these terms.

In order to emphasize the speed necessary for such a dispatch, the *Targum* tells us that these horses were *richsa*, "racing horses." While also wanting to focus the reader's attention on the speed with which the order had to be distributed, Rashi explains the uncommon word *haachasht'ranim* (royal) as "speedy camels accustomed to race."

Noting parallels in the Arabic usage, Ibn Ezra's explanation is closer to the *Targum*. For Ibn Ezra, these are "royal horses unlike any other."

ח:יא אֲשֶׁר נָתַן הַמֶּלֶךְ לַיְּהוּדִים אֲשֶׁר בְּכָל־עִיר־וָעִיר לְהִקָּהֵל וְלַעֲמֹד עַל־נַפְשָׁם לְהַשְׁמִיד וְלַהֲרֹג וּלְאַבֵּד אֶת־כָּל־חֵיל עַם וּמְדִינָה הַצָּרִים אֹתָם טַף וְנָשִׁים וּשְׁלָלָם לָבוֹז:

8:11 "THE KING HAS PERMITTED THE JEWS IN EACH AND EVERY CITY TO GATHER TOGETHER TO DEFEND THEMSELVES AND TO UTTERLY DESTROY ANY ARMED FORCE, WHETHER BELONGING TO A PEOPLE OR BELONGING TO A PROVINCE, THAT MIGHT ATTACK THEM, THEIR SPOUSES, OR THEIR CHILDREN, AND PLUNDER THE POSSESSIONS OF THEIR ENEMIES.

This verse articulates the new order that is being rapidly distributed throughout the kingdom. Since the original order still stands, the king needs to give another order that will permit to the Jewish people the only possible way to respond to the upcoming attack. The Jewish people are not only being given the right to self-defense, they are also given the right to establish local militias to protect themselves, their families, and their communities.

We choose to translate the three verbs *l'hashmid* (to destroy), *l'harog* (to kill), and *l'abeid* (to annihilate) as "to utterly destroy." While this verse seems to fulfill the literary needs of the story and provides a response to what was already set in motion, it presents the contemporary reader with an ethical paradox to resolve. The construction of the verse makes unclear as to whose spouses, children, or possessions are being threatened. Does this verse give the Jewish people the right to defend their spouses, children, and possessions, or does it give them permission to destroy the spouses, children, and possessions of their enemies? While families (especially women and children) have become all too commonplace as targets of war, it would seem too harsh to be placed in a book in the Bible, especially if the Jewish people are the ones doing the targeting. (See Deuteronomy 2:34, for example.) The classic commentators provide no assistance in this regard. Given our sense of Jewish history and Jewish ethics, we choose to construe the words as referring to the Jewish people defending their families, rather than to attacking those of their enemies.

ח:יב בְּיוֹם אֶחָד בְּכָל־מְדִינוֹת הַמֶּלֶךְ אֲחַשְׁוֵרוֹשׁ בִּשְׁלוֹשָׁה עָשָׂר לְחֹדֶשׁ שְׁנֵים־עָשָׂר הוּא־חֹדֶשׁ אֲדָר:

8:12 "THIS WILL OCCUR THROUGHOUT THE PROVINCES OF KING AHASUERUS ON ONE DAY, THE THIRTEENTH DAY OF ADAR, THE TWELFTH MONTH."

This verse is simply the continuation of the royal order that began in the previous verse.

ח:יג פַּתְשֶׁגֶן הַכְּתָב לְהִנָּתֵן דָּת בְּכָל־מְדִינָה וּמְדִינָה גָּלוּי לְכָל־הָעַמִּים וְלִהְיוֹת הַיְּהוּדִים עֲתִידִים לַיּוֹם הַזֶּה לְהִנָּקֵם מֵאֹיְבֵיהֶם:

8:13 A COPY OF THE ROYAL ORDER WAS PUBLISHED AS LAW IN EVERY PROVINCE AND WAS PROCLAIMED TO EVERY PEOPLE THAT JEWS ON THAT DAY WOULD TAKE REVENGE AGAINST THEIR ENEMIES.

Following the order of the king, the new law is widely distributed, giving permission to the Jewish people of ancient Persia to defend themselves against their enemies. This order seems to go beyond the original decree. It seems that the Jewish people are permitted to anticipate the evil intent of their enemies and preemptively destroy them. One might assume that upon reading the second order, even those who might have followed the directive of the first order would cease and desist. Because of the apparent hatred that Haman had sown among the people, this second order allows the Jewish people to rise up against their enemies without any provocation. The Jews would still be in danger, since the local Persians so hated them that they might have attacked anyway.

ח:יד הָרָצִים רֹכְבֵי הָרֶכֶשׁ הָאֲחַשְׁתְּרָנִים יָצְאוּ מְבֹהָלִים וּדְחוּפִים
בִּדְבַר הַמֶּלֶךְ וְהַדָּת נִתְּנָה בְּשׁוּשַׁן הַבִּירָה:

8:14 Riding on relay horses, the couriers sped out, spurred by the king's command. And the decree was published in the fortress of Shushan.

The couriers follow the king's orders and ride quickly to make sure that the king's decree is issued widely as he requested. In the *Targum*'s translation of the verse, which emphasizes the haste with which the couriers race, they ride *artulyanei* (naked or lightly armed). (See Jastrow, p. 1116.) Apparently, as representatives of the king, this was usually not the case.

ח:טו וּמָרְדֳּכַי יָצָא מִלִּפְנֵי הַמֶּלֶךְ בִּלְבוּשׁ מַלְכוּת תְּכֵלֶת וָחוּר וַעֲטֶרֶת
זָהָב גְּדוֹלָה וְתַכְרִיךְ בּוּץ וְאַרְגָּמָן וְהָעִיר שׁוּשָׁן צָהֲלָה וְשָׂמֵחָה:

8:15 Mordecai went out from the king's presence attired in royal robes of blue and white, with a large golden crown on his head, and a cloak of white linen and purple wool around his body. The city of Shushan was filled with rejoicing.

Anyone who sees Mordecai dressed this way knows immediately that he is favored by the king—and should therefore be given similar respect. We follow Koehler-Baumgartner (p. 115) and combine linen and white fabric to become "white linen." We also follow the same source (p. 84) in translating *argaman* as "purple wool."

The *Targum* doesn't seem to be able to refrain from celebrating Mordecai's victory over Haman and the victory ride that comes as a result. So its translation of this verse is rather extensive. To begin, Mordecai is *chadei v'shapir l'beih biykara sagi*, "happy and very cheerful," because he is given the unusual honor of wearing royal garments. In addition to the clothing and accessories described in the verse, the *Targum* suggests that "the crown was made of the gold of Ophir [see Job 22:24], studded with pearls and precious stones." His "pants were greenish blue." "Images of every kind of plumed bird and every bird that flies in the heaven" adorned the purple cloak. The cloak was also "adorned by 120 talents of gold, in which grooves were made that beryl might be set in them. On his feet were Parthian (red) socks and Macedonian gilt shoes sealed with emeralds. A sword of Median steel, supported by a golden chain inscribed with a picture of Jerusalem, was about his waist. A symbol of Mehuzah [a large Jewish trading town on the Tigris] was on the handle of the sword. Different colors were on the point of the sword. A golden ornament was on the golden crown on Mordecai's head indicating to anyone who saw it that Mordecai was a Jew. This fulfilled the words of the verse, 'All the peoples of the earth shall see that the name of the Eternal is proclaimed about you' (Deuteronomy 28:10)."

In addition to depicting Mordecai's regal outfit, the *Targum* makes a number of strong statements about what happens once Mordecai leaves the royal gate. "An announcement accompanied by trumpet blasts was made by the priests that whoever would not become subservient to Mordecai and the Jews would be chopped to pieces and his house destroyed." Apparently, "the ten sons of Haman clasped their hands and sang before Mordecai, praising the One who had rewarded the Jews and requited their enemies. They added that their father had been a fool who had depended on his wealth and his honor.

"Humble Mordecai was weakened by his fasting and his prayers. Righteous Esther gazed through the window [since it was inappropriate for a queen to walk through the streets in public]. When Mordecai saw her, he said to her, 'Praised be the One who did not give me over as prey food to their teeth.' Esther answered, 'My help is from *Adonai*, who made heaven and earth (Psalm 121:2).' Those on high rejoice at the downfall of wicked Haman and praise the salvation that was afforded the Jews and the honor given to Mordecai the righteous at that time."

To help readers get a better sense of the clothes Mordecai wore, Rashi explains that *tachrich* is the kind of cloak made of linen in which one wraps oneself. Ibn Ezra explains that this word is found in ancient texts and it is like a cloak. He also notes that *butz* is a fine and expensive linen that comes from Egypt. Ibn Ezra notes that Shushan is mentioned in this verse—since it doesn't seem to follow the flow of the text—because it was a city with a large Jewish population. He also explains that *tzahalah* (lightening up), which we translate as "filled with rejoicing," signifies the kind of illumination that might come to a person sitting in darkness who then goes out into the light.

ח:טז לַיְּהוּדִים הָיְתָה אוֹרָה וְשִׂמְחָה וְשָׂשֹׂן וִיקָר:

8:16 THERE WAS LIGHT AND JOY, HAPPINESS AND HONOR
FOR THE JEWS.

This verse may be familiar, because it has found its way into the *Havdalah* ritual that
marks the conclusion of the Sabbath. In its pietistic translation, the *Targum* explains
that the "joy" was because "the Jews had the authority to study Torah, to keep the
Sabbath and the Festivals, to circumcise their sons, and to put *t'fillin* on their arms and
heads."

ח:יז וּבְכָל־מְדִינָה וּמְדִינָה וּבְכָל־עִיר וָעִיר מְקוֹם אֲשֶׁר דְּבַר־הַמֶּלֶךְ
וְדָתוֹ מַגִּיעַ שִׂמְחָה וְשָׂשֹׂן לַיְּהוּדִים מִשְׁתֶּה וְיוֹם טוֹב וְרַבִּים
מֵעַמֵּי הָאָרֶץ מִתְיַהֲדִים כִּי־נָפַל פַּחַד־הַיְּהוּדִים עֲלֵיהֶם:

8:17 IN EVERY PROVINCE AND IN EVERY CITY, WHEREVER THE
KING'S COMMAND AND DECREE CAME, THERE WAS JOY
AND GLADNESS FOR THE JEWS: A FEAST AND A HOLIDAY.
MANY OF THE PEOPLE OF THE LAND PRETENDED TO BE
JEWISH BECAUSE FEAR OF THE JEWS HAD FALLEN ON
THEM.

The Jewish people have known circumstances similar to those described in this verse
throughout their history. Many Jews in many places have had to pretend to be non-
Jews in order to survive. As a result, it is troubling to find this statement in a Jewish
sacred text. One would like to believe that, because the Jewish people frequently had
to live through such experiences, they would not create the milieu in which someone
else had to do so.

Rashi explains that the word *mityahadim*, which we translate as "pretended to be
Jewish," actually means that people converted to Judaism. For Ibn Ezra, this word is
strange, particularly from a grammatical point of view, since it is a verb made from a
noun: *Y'hudah* (the name Judah) or *Y'hudi* (Jew). To support the possibility, Ibn Ezra
quotes an earlier grammarian, Rabbi Judah, who suggests that the word *tormim* (offer)
comes from *t'rumah* (offering).

Gold of Ophir

Ophir was one of the sons of Joktan who settled in southern Arabia (Genesis 10:26–29). Solomon's ships traded with Ophir. Gold in Ophir was plentiful and considered to be of superior quality because of its purity. Thus, the gold of Ophir became an idiom to reflect the best gold or anything of exceptional value (Psalm 45:10; Isaiah 13:12; I Chronicles 29:3–4).

GLEANINGS

Humor, the Language of Faith

On Purim, the laughter reaches surprising heights. This forces some consideration of the role of humor in religion in general. Purim is a put-on in many ways: witness the broad caricature of the Megillah and the raucousness of the celebration. The humor carries a religious message, however. Humor expresses transcendence of unredeemed reality, and it takes sanctity itself with a sense of limits. Satire prevents us from making the sacred absolute (only God is absolute). The unchecked tendency to respect religion all too often leads to deifying the ritual and the outward form of God. If people take the sacred too solemnly, they are confusing their religious expression—which is relative and limited in truth—with the infinite God whom they really seek to serve.

There is another element involved, an element one can appreciate a bit more in the generation after the Holocaust. The humor is in part a defiance and an outcry. . . .

One can only respond with laughter and mockery and put-on, satirizing God and the bitter joke this world threatens to become. It is enough to drive a person to drink! (Jews act this out.) But as the hilarity reaches its climax, Jews move beyond bitterness to humor. In laughing at religious forms and at reality, one admits the fallibility of religious hopes but one also affirms them. In satire and humor, the pretensions of the moment are punctured. Through the humor, Jews project themselves into future redeemed reality that transcends the moment. Thus, hope is kept alive and the Messiah remains possible.

Irving Greenberg, *The Jewish Way: Living the Holidays*
(New York: Simon & Schuster, 1988), 254

The Primary Sacredness of Jewish Survival

We are what we believe, and for as long as I can remember, my fundamental beliefs have been these: the primary sacredness of Jewish survival, both for the Jews as a people and for humanity at large; the value of every single Jewish life, especially now, in the aftermath of Hitler's genocidal attack; the inestimable value of Israel as a physical and spiritual center; the responsibility of every Jew for every other and for the homeland. . . .

I believe in the uniqueness of the Jewish people.

Jews share the quality of humanness with all others on this planet, yet we are different in many ways. And if we were not, we probably would have disappeared, as have all the others who started on the path of history when we did, almost four millennia ago. There are two elements in our individuality: the circumstances of our birth at Mt. Sinai, where we were linked to God and a moral code; and our acceptance of an eternal mission, through the concept of redemption by a Messiah, in which a better world will be born for all humans to enjoy.

I believe in the centrality of a specific land—Israel.

The moral covenant that marked our beginning and the Messianic redemption that will mark our ending are both connected to that small sliver of sacred space at the confluence of three continents. There we wrote the most significant book known to the human race and spawned two globe-girdling daughter religions. The homeland was gained and lost, gained and lost again, but the yearning for it has provided the strength to endure the endless trials of the centuries. Now the land has been gained yet another time, in our era, and, we hope, for *all* time. How miraculous!

I believe in Judaism's gift to humanity.

Along with our separateness and particularity as a special people, we also possess a quality of universalism in its fullest measure. We stress and express, in word and hopefully in deed, the equality of all persons. Our sacred literature teaches that all

130

human beings come from one God. The moral injunctions of our prophets repeatedly state that the stranger shall be treated as the native-born, and the messianic vision of peace, plenty, and health embraces all humankind, not just the Hebrews.

I believe in the Diaspora.

The dispersal of the Jewish people across time and space is an integral part of its creative genius. The Diaspora has been a fruitful hinterland providing intellectual spark and charismatic personalities. At present, the American Jewish future appears cloudy, even dark. But if it brightens, and American Jews maintain their Jewish identity in the midst of unprecedented freedom and affluence, the Diaspora of the future may outstrip all previous ones in achievement.

Herbert A. Friedman, *Roots of the Future*
(Jerusalem: Geffen Publishing House, 1999), 17–18

CHAPTER NINE

ט:א וּבִשְׁנֵים עָשָׂר חֹדֶשׁ הוּא־חֹדֶשׁ אֲדָר בִּשְׁלוֹשָׁה עָשָׂר יוֹם בּוֹ אֲשֶׁר הִגִּיעַ דְּבַר־הַמֶּלֶךְ וְדָתוֹ לְהֵעָשׂוֹת בַּיּוֹם אֲשֶׁר שִׂבְּרוּ אֹיְבֵי הַיְּהוּדִים לִשְׁלוֹט בָּהֶם וְנַהֲפוֹךְ הוּא אֲשֶׁר יִשְׁלְטוּ הַיְּהוּדִים הֵמָּה בְּשֹׂנְאֵיהֶם:

9:1 SO ON THE THIRTEENTH DAY OF THE TWELFTH MONTH, THE MONTH OF ADAR, THE DAY WHEN THE ORDER OF THE KING WAS TO BE CARRIED OUT, ON THE VERY DAY WHEN THE ENEMIES OF THE JEWS HAD HOPED TO HAVE THE JEWS IN THEIR POWER, THE REVERSE HAPPENED AND THE JEWS HAD THEIR ENEMIES IN THEIR POWER.

This chapter initiates a discussion about the enemies of the Jewish people. In so doing, it extends the lessons of the Book of Esther considerably. While this verse seems straightforward and describes the turn of events that was anticipated by previous verses, the *Targum* explains and elaborates on the reason and origin for the change of events. This is particularly important because the author of the Book of Esther does not mention the role of God in the story. The *Targum*, on the other hand, attributes the reversal of fortune as coming from heaven as a result of the merit of Abraham. This notion of *z'chut avot*, the merit that is credited to our ancestors from which later generations benefit, is a common theme in Rabbinic literature. Because of Abraham's goodness, we merit God's favor—and intervention.

ט:ב נִקְהֲלוּ הַיְּהוּדִים בְּעָרֵיהֶם בְּכָל־מְדִינוֹת הַמֶּלֶךְ אֲחַשְׁוֵרוֹשׁ לִשְׁלֹחַ יָד בִּמְבַקְשֵׁי רָעָתָם וְאִישׁ לֹא־עָמַד לִפְנֵיהֶם כִּי־נָפַל פַּחְדָּם עַל־כָּל־הָעַמִּים:

9:2 In every city, in all the provinces of King Ahasuerus, the Jews gathered together to attack those who wished to wrong them. No one could withstand them, because a dread of them [the Jewish people] fell upon all peoples.

Suddenly, all the various peoples who are citizens of ancient Persia are afraid of the Jews. However difficult it is from a modern ethical perspective to read this verse and those that follow, later readers of this text who found themselves in life-threatening situations may have found hope in it.

ט:ג וְכָל־שָׂרֵי הַמְּדִינוֹת וְהָאֲחַשְׁדַּרְפְּנִים וְהַפַּחוֹת וְעֹשֵׂי הַמְּלָאכָה אֲשֶׁר לַמֶּלֶךְ מְנַשְּׂאִים אֶת־הַיְּהוּדִים כִּי־נָפַל פַּחַד־מָרְדֳּכַי עֲלֵיהֶם:

9:3 Because they were now afraid of Mordecai, all the officials of the provinces—the satraps, the governors, and the supervisors—began to favor the Jews.

This verse continues the story of the new position in which the Jews of ancient Persia find themselves. It is out of fear that the people of the kingdom look more favorably upon the Jewish people. The victim becomes the aggressor. Reveling in turning the tables is unseemly, but as a victimized people (reading this under difficult circumstances), the Jews—and the author—are fantasizing about being in a position of power.

ט:ד כִּי־גָדוֹל מָרְדֳּכַי בְּבֵית הַמֶּלֶךְ וְשָׁמְעוֹ הוֹלֵךְ בְּכָל־הַמְּדִינוֹת כִּי־
הָאִישׁ מָרְדֳּכַי הוֹלֵךְ וְגָדוֹל:

9:4 Because of his influence in the royal palace,
Mordecai became more and more powerful. His
fame spread throughout all of the provinces.

Suddenly, Esther's role is eclipsed by Mordecai's fame. The *Targum* spells out the
reasons why Mordecai becomes influential. Apparently, he takes on a number of roles
in the royal household, becoming an administrator (*apotropos*; the Greek word
epitropus has the same meaning), a master, and an officer. The *Targum* also explains
the extent of Mordecai's fame: coins with his image on them are to be found throughout the provinces of the kingdom.

Ibn Ezra notes that the phrase *holeich v'gadol* (literally, "going and big") is an idiom
for "became more powerful." It is transformed into an idiom by using a verb in its
simple form (what linguists call *kal*) with an adjective to develop its meaning.

ט:ה וַיַּכּוּ הַיְּהוּדִים בְּכָל־אֹיְבֵיהֶם מַכַּת־חֶרֶב וְהֶרֶג וְאַבְדָן וַיַּעֲשׂוּ
בְשֹׂנְאֵיהֶם כִּרְצוֹנָם:

9:5 The Jews struck down their enemies with the
sword, killing and destroying them and doing
whatever they wanted to their enemies.

While these words are read aloud when the entire Scroll of Esther is read during the
public celebration of Purim, it is clear why they are sometimes excluded from a literal
translation of the text. Some are disturbed by the ferocity with which the Jewish
people took vengeance on their enemies. Perhaps this is one of the reasons why so
many emphasize the possibility that the Book of Esther may be a work of fiction.
Thus, the vengeance that is described would never have taken place. It could also be
that those who read it couldn't believe that the Jewish people would be in such a
position of power. The *Targum*, however, goes so far as to add *k'tilat golmin* (death by
stoning) to its catalogue of killing and explains *v'avdan* (and destroying them) as
v'hovad nafshata (and destruction of life) in order to leave no doubt as to the extent of
the bloodshed.

ט:ו וּבְשׁוּשַׁן הַבִּירָה הָרְגוּ הַיְּהוּדִים וְאַבֵּד חֲמֵשׁ מֵאוֹת אִישׁ:

9:6 THE JEWS KILLED FIVE HUNDRED MEN IN THE FORTRESS
CITY OF SHUSHAN.

While the Hebrew includes *v'abeid* (and destroying) in order to link this verse to the previous one, we do not translate the term, since we do not believe that it adds any meaning to the verse. Regardless, this repetition emphasizes the utter destruction that is undertaken and the extent to which the Jews endeavor to destroy any trace (and future seed) of their enemy. The *Targum* tells us that those who were killed were *rufilin*, part of the "military tribunes of the House of Amalek," the historical enemies of the Jewish people.

ט:ז וְאֵת פַּרְשַׁנְדָּתָא וְאֵת דַּלְפוֹן וְאֵת אַסְפָּתָא:

9:7 THEY ALSO KILLED PARSHANDATHA, DALPHON, AND
ASPATHA.

This verse begins the list of the names of the ten sons of Haman. It is customary during the public reading of the *M'gillah* to recite the names of Haman's sons in one breath.

ט:ח וְאֵת פּוֹרָתָא וְאֵת אֲדַלְיָא וְאֵת אֲרִידָתָא:

ט:ט וְאֵת פַּרְמַשְׁתָּא וְאֵת אֲרִיסַי וְאֵת אֲרִידַי וְאֵת וַיְזָתָא:

ט:י עֲשֶׂרֶת בְּנֵי הָמָן בֶּן־הַמְּדָתָא צֹרֵר הַיְּהוּדִים הָרְגוּ וּבַבִּזָּה לֹא
שָׁלְחוּ אֶת־יָדָם:

9:8 PORATHA, ADALIA, AND ARIDATHA.

9:9 PARMASHTA, ARISAI, ARIDAI, AND VAIZATHA.

9:10 ALTHOUGH THEY KILLED THE TEN SONS OF HAMAN, THE
ENEMY OF THE JEWS, THEY TOOK NO PLUNDER.

As if to mitigate the nature of the act, the author implies that this killing is just revenge, or perhaps even self-defense, the evidence of which is that no property is taken.

Rashi cites a book of mysticism called *Seder Olam*, which identifies the ten sons of Haman as those enemies of the Jews who had written a letter of accusation against the inhabitants of Judah and Jerusalem as reported in Ezra 4:6. Rashi tells the reader that the letter, the text of which is given in Ezra 4:8–16, was written to impede the rebuilding of the Temple by those who were leaving Babylonian captivity. As Ezra 4:24 indicates, the letter was successful and the rebuilding of the Temple ceased.

Rashi tells us that the Jewish people did not plunder the Persians because they were afraid that the king would be displeased by a loss of money—and his potential revenue. Ibn Ezra suggests that the Jewish people realized that it would end up in the royal treasury anyhow, so why bother?

ט:יא בַּיּוֹם הַהוּא בָּא מִסְפַּר הַהֲרוּגִים בְּשׁוּשַׁן הַבִּירָה לִפְנֵי הַמֶּלֶךְ:

9:11 THE NUMBER OF THOSE KILLED IN THE FORTRESS CITY OF SHUSHAN WAS REPORTED TO THE KING ON THE SAME DAY.

Just as the news of the king's decree travels quickly throughout the kingdom, so too does the news of the loss of life of his subjects.

ט:יב וַיֹּאמֶר הַמֶּלֶךְ לְאֶסְתֵּר הַמַּלְכָּה בְּשׁוּשַׁן הַבִּירָה הָרְגוּ הַיְּהוּדִים וְאַבֵּד חֲמֵשׁ מֵאוֹת אִישׁ וְאֵת עֲשֶׂרֶת בְּנֵי־הָמָן בִּשְׁאָר מְדִינוֹת הַמֶּלֶךְ מֶה עָשׂוּ וּמַה־שְּׁאֵלָתֵךְ וְיִנָּתֵן לָךְ וּמַה־בַּקָּשָׁתֵךְ עוֹד וְתֵעָשׂ:

9:12 THE KING THEN SAID TO QUEEN ESTHER, "IF IN THE FORTRESS CITY OF SHUSHAN, THE JEWS KILLED FIVE HUNDRED MEN AND ALSO THE TEN SONS OF HAMAN, THEN WHAT MUST THEY HAVE DONE IN THE OTHER ROYAL PROVINCES? WHAT ELSE DO YOU WANT? IT WILL BE GIVEN TO YOU. WHAT ELSE DO YOU WISH? IT WILL BE DONE."

At first, it seems that the king is alarmed by what took place in Shushan and is afraid to imagine what has happened throughout the kingdom. But he is still enamored by

Esther and is prepared to give her whatever she wants. If the Jewish people are bold enough to kill important people such as the sons of Haman in the realm's capital, where political power resides, then one can only imagine what havoc could be wrought outside of direct royal control.

Just as we omitted translating *v'abeid* in 9:6, we have also not translated it here.

ט:יג וַתֹּאמֶר אֶסְתֵּר אִם־עַל־הַמֶּלֶךְ טוֹב יִנָּתֵן גַּם־מָחָר לַיְּהוּדִים אֲשֶׁר בְּשׁוּשָׁן לַעֲשׂוֹת כְּדָת הַיּוֹם וְאֵת עֲשֶׂרֶת בְּנֵי־הָמָן יִתְלוּ עַל־הָעֵץ׃

9:13 ESTHER ANSWERED, "IF IT PLEASE THE KING, LET THE JEWS IN SHUSHAN DO TOMORROW WHAT THEY DID TODAY. AND LET THEM HANG THE CORPSES OF THE TEN SONS OF HAMAN ON THE GALLOWS."

It seems that Esther is complicit in the killing even if she does not kill anyone herself. While the Hebrew doesn't explicitly say so, we follow Rashi and add "the corpses" to our translation of the Hebrew text, since the ten sons of Haman are already dead at this point in the narrative.

These last chapters of the Book of Esther portray the Jews as extremely bloodthirsty. They may not be what the average reader of Esther would like to read (and it is certainly not the story of Esther that is usually taught to children). We read the Book of Esther because we want to celebrate the happy holiday of Purim. The vengeful last chapters challenge not only our sense of the book but also our sense of ourselves. However, not to present them with translation or not to present them at all (as is the case in many editions) belies the text.

The *Targum* softens the verse by having Esther ask the king to allow the Jewish people to have a holiday filled with joy to celebrate the miracle of their deliverance. Nevertheless, the verse includes the hanging of the ten sons of Haman.

ט:יד וַיֹּאמֶר הַמֶּלֶךְ לְהֵעָשׂוֹת כֵּן וַתִּנָּתֵן דָּת בְּשׁוּשָׁן וְאֵת עֲשֶׂרֶת בְּנֵי־
הָמָן תָּלוּ:

9:14 THE KING COMMANDED THAT IT BE DONE: THE LAW
WAS PUBLISHED IN SHUSHAN. SO THEY HANGED THE
CORPSES OF THE TEN SONS OF HAMAN.

As we learned earlier in the book, the king's directives are written down and distributed as law. The king fulfills Esther's wish, and the corpses of Haman's sons are put
on public display. As we did in the previous verse, we add ''the corpses'' to our
translation of the Hebrew text.

ט:טו וַיִּקָּהֲלוּ הַיְּהוּדִים אֲשֶׁר־בְּשׁוּשָׁן גַּם בְּיוֹם אַרְבָּעָה עָשָׂר לְחֹדֶשׁ
אֲדָר וַיַּהַרְגוּ בְשׁוּשָׁן שְׁלֹשׁ מֵאוֹת אִישׁ וּבַבִּזָּה לֹא שָׁלְחוּ אֶת־יָדָם:

9:15 ON THE FOURTEENTH OF ADAR, THE JEWS OF
SHUSHAN GATHERED AGAIN IN THE CITY AND KILLED
THREE HUNDRED MEN. HOWEVER, THEY TOOK NO
PLUNDER.

More death. And again, to emphasize the ethical nature of these killings, the reader is
reminded that no plunder is taken in this episode either. Apparently the Jewish people
had scattered after their previous acts and had to reconnoiter. By identifying the three
hundred men as belonging to the House of Amalek, the *Targum* shows the reader that
they were both the natural enemies of the Jewish people and related to Haman.

ט:טז וּשְׁאָר הַיְּהוּדִים אֲשֶׁר בִּמְדִינוֹת הַמֶּלֶךְ נִקְהֲלוּ וְעָמֹד עַל־נַפְשָׁם
וְנוֹחַ מֵאֹיְבֵיהֶם וְהָרוֹג בְּשֹׂנְאֵיהֶם חֲמִשָּׁה וְשִׁבְעִים אָלֶף וּבַבִּזָּה
לֹא שָׁלְחוּ אֶת־יָדָם:

9:16 THE REST OF THE JEWS LIVING IN THE ROYAL PROVINCES
GATHERED TO DEFEND THEMSELVES. THEY DEFEATED
THEIR ENEMIES, KILLING SEVENTY-FIVE THOUSAND OF
THEIR FOES, BUT TAKING NO PLUNDER.

Yet more killing. And still no plunder. While one might be able to rationalize the previous killings as self-defense, it is clear that this represents a vast destruction of human life that is hard to justify under any circumstances.

ט:יז בְּיוֹם־שְׁלוֹשָׁה עָשָׂר לְחֹדֶשׁ אֲדָר וְנוֹחַ בְּאַרְבָּעָה עָשָׂר בּוֹ וְעָשֹׂה
אֹתוֹ יוֹם מִשְׁתֶּה וְשִׂמְחָה:

9:17 THIS HAPPENED ON THE THIRTEENTH OF ADAR. ON
THE FOURTEENTH OF ADAR, THEY RESTED AND MADE IT
A DAY OF FEASTING AND JOY.

This verse helps us identify the reason behind the dating of the Purim celebration that will be affirmed in the next verse.

The *Targum's* translation of the verse offers us the reason behind such an extensive killing spree: "the killing of the seed of Amalek."

ט:יח וְהַיְּהוּדִים אֲשֶׁר־בְּשׁוּשָׁן נִקְהֲלוּ בִּשְׁלוֹשָׁה עָשָׂר בּוֹ וּבְאַרְבָּעָה
עָשָׂר בּוֹ וְנוֹחַ בַּחֲמִשָּׁה עָשָׂר בּוֹ וְעָשֹׁה אֹתוֹ יוֹם מִשְׁתֶּה וְשִׂמְחָה:

9:18 THE JEWS WHO LIVED IN SHUSHAN HAD GATHERED
TOGETHER ON THE THIRTEENTH AND FOURTEENTH AND
HAD RESTED ON THE FIFTEENTH. HENCE, THEY MADE
THAT DAY [AS THE DAY] OF FEASTING AND JOY.

It is not clear from this verse why the Jews assemble. The *Targum* says that it is "to
destroy the seed of Amalek." It is either a reference to previous verses or perhaps an
indication that more killing takes place that is not described by the author.

ט:יט עַל־כֵּן הַיְּהוּדִים הַפְּרָזִים הַיּשְׁבִים בְּעָרֵי הַפְּרָזוֹת עֹשִׂים אֵת יוֹם
אַרְבָּעָה עָשָׂר לְחֹדֶשׁ אֲדָר שִׂמְחָה וּמִשְׁתֶּה וְיוֹם טוֹב וּמִשְׁלוֹחַ
מָנוֹת אִישׁ לְרֵעֵהוּ:

9:19 THIS IS WHY RURAL JEWS LIVING IN THE OPEN TOWNS
OBSERVE THE FOURTEENTH OF ADAR AS A DAY OF JOY
AND FEASTING, A HOLIDAY TO SEND GIFTS TO ONE
ANOTHER.

This verse confirms the dating of Purim. It also provides the rationale for the custom of
mishlo-ach manot, "sending packages" to friends and relatives for Purim. We follow
Koehler-Baumgartner (p. 965) in our translation of the uncommon adjective *hap'razim*
(country folk, rural) and the combination of the construct *arei* (cities of) and the uncommon noun *hap'razot* (the open country) as "the open towns." The *Targum* translates *hap'razim* as *patzicha-ei* (inhabitants of walled cities) and *arei hap'razot* as *kirvei
fatzichaya* (unwalled cities). This helps us to understand the distinction that both the
Book of Esther and the Mishnah (*M'gillah* 1:1) make between the celebration of Purim
in walled cities (like Jerusalem) on the day that follows its celebration everywhere else.

ט:כ וַיִּכְתֹּב מָרְדֳּכַי אֶת־הַדְּבָרִים הָאֵלֶּה וַיִּשְׁלַח סְפָרִים אֶל־כָּל־
הַיְּהוּדִים אֲשֶׁר בְּכָל־מְדִינוֹת הַמֶּלֶךְ אֲחַשְׁוֵרוֹשׁ הַקְּרוֹבִים
וְהָרְחוֹקִים:

**9:20 MORDECAI RECORDED THESE EVENTS AND SENT LETTERS
TO THE JEWS OF THE ROYAL PROVINCES, NEAR AND FAR,**

While the purpose of Mordecai's recording these events and then distributing them is
not clear, Ibn Ezra suggests that it is to order the celebration of Purim for the next year
and those following.

ט:כא לְקַיֵּם עֲלֵיהֶם לִהְיוֹת עֹשִׂים אֵת יוֹם אַרְבָּעָה עָשָׂר לְחֹדֶשׁ אֲדָר
וְאֵת יוֹם־חֲמִשָּׁה עָשָׂר בּוֹ בְּכָל־שָׁנָה וְשָׁנָה:

**9:21 TO HAVE THEM OBSERVE THE FOURTEENTH AND
FIFTEENTH OF THE MONTH OF ADAR EVERY YEAR**

This is a continuation of the previous verse. The *Targum* wants to make more explicit
the directive contained in the verse so that its readers "fulfill the order of the law
imposed on them to observe the fourteenth and fifteenth of Adar every year."

ט:כב כַּיָּמִים אֲשֶׁר־נָחוּ בָהֶם הַיְּהוּדִים מֵאֹיְבֵיהֶם וְהַחֹדֶשׁ אֲשֶׁר נֶהְפַּךְ
לָהֶם מִיָּגוֹן לְשִׂמְחָה וּמֵאֵבֶל לְיוֹם טוֹב לַעֲשׂוֹת אוֹתָם יְמֵי מִשְׁתֶּה
וְשִׂמְחָה וּמִשְׁלֹחַ מָנוֹת אִישׁ לְרֵעֵהוּ וּמַתָּנוֹת לָאֶבְיֹנִים:

**9:22 AS THE DAYS WHEN THE JEWS DEFEATED THEIR ENEMIES
AND THE MONTH THAT FOR THEM HAD CHANGED FROM
GRIEF TO JOY AND FROM MOURNING TO CELEBRATION.
THEY WERE TO OBSERVE THEM AS DAYS OF FEASTING
AND JOY AND THE SENDING OF GIFTS TO ONE ANOTHER
AND PRESENTS TO THE POOR.**

This verse gives both the rationale for the imperative of the preceding verses, as well
as some specific direction as to how to observe the festival. The *Targum* wants to

clarify the instructions even further. It adds *umaaha d'tzidkata* (coins, funds, of charity) to what is considered to be "presents to the poor."

Ibn Ezra feels that the mention of "the month" requires explanation. Since the Jewish calendar is a soli-lunar calendar, if there are two months of Adar—as there are during a leap year—Purim ought to fall on the month next to Nisan (that is, II Adar). He notes that other interpreters incorrectly argue the reverse (that is, I Adar) but contends that the mentioning of "the month" in this verse substantiates his position. Otherwise, why would "the month" be mentioned if the position were obvious? Today, Purim is indeed celebrated in II Adar.

ט:כג וְקִבֵּל הַיְּהוּדִים אֵת אֲשֶׁר־הֵחֵלּוּ לַעֲשׂוֹת וְאֵת אֲשֶׁר־כָּתַב מָרְדֳּכַי אֲלֵיהֶם:

9:23 THE JEWS TOOK UPON THEMSELVES TO CONTINUE WHAT THEY HAD BEGUN, WHAT MORDECAI HAD DIRECTED THEM TO DO.

Since the first word of the verse *v'kibeil* (received, accepted) is written in the singular, the *Targum* believes that it requires explanation. Thus, it adds *kulhon...kachada* (all of them as one). This indicates that "all the Jews as one took upon themselves to continue...."

ט:כד כִּי הָמָן בֶּן־הַמְּדָתָא הָאֲגָגִי צֹרֵר כָּל־הַיְּהוּדִים חָשַׁב עַל־הַיְּהוּדִים לְאַבְּדָם וְהִפִּיל פּוּר הוּא הַגּוֹרָל לְהֻמָּם וּלְאַבְּדָם:

9:24 FOR HAMAN, SON OF HAMMEDATHA, THE AGAGITE HAD PLOTTED TO DESTROY ALL THE JEWS AND HAD CAST *PUR* [A LOT], FOR THEIR DEBASEMENT AND DESTRUCTION.

This verse begins a summary of the Book of Esther. In it, the author attempts to explain the name of this festival and the reason behind it as related to the word for "lots" (*pur*). Haman's name is mentioned once again so that there should be no misunderstanding as to who was responsible for the plot against the Jews. Rashi claims that *haman ben ham'data* (clearly an alliteration) is used to indicate that Haman, the villain, wanted *l'humam* (to throw them into confusion) and "to destroy them."

ט:כה וּבְבֹאָהּ לִפְנֵי הַמֶּלֶךְ אָמַר עִם־הַסֵּפֶר יָשׁוּב מַחֲשַׁבְתּוֹ הָרָעָה אֲשֶׁר־חָשַׁב עַל־הַיְּהוּדִים עַל־רֹאשׁוֹ וְתָלוּ אֹתוֹ וְאֶת־בָּנָיו עַל־הָעֵץ:

9:25 BUT WHEN SHE [ESTHER] CAME BEFORE THE KING, HE GAVE ORAL AND WRITTEN ORDERS THAT THE EVIL SCHEME THAT HE [HAMAN] PLOTTED AGAINST THE JEWS BE TURNED AGAINST HIM, SO THAT HE AND HIS TEN SONS WERE HANGED ON THE GALLOWS.

This is not an easy verse to translate. The first word, a verb with a prefix, *b'voah* (literally, "in her coming") does not indicate who or what came. We have followed the *Targum*, Rashi, and Ibn Ezra in assuming that the word is a reference to Esther. Next, after the word *amar* (he said), are the words *im hasefer* (with the book). It is not clear which book this is referring to. The *Targum* does not translate the words at all. In our translation, we have followed Rashi, who explains that "the king spoke orally and commanded that orders be written." In this way, the king's oral orders are translated into written orders. Both are considered law. Third, *amar im hasefer* is followed by *yashuv machashavto haraah* (let return his evil thoughts). We have translated the phrase as "that the evil scheme . . . be turned against him."

For Ibn Ezra, the "turning against" refers more to the king's decree, which was recalled, rather than Haman's plot.

ט:כו עַל־כֵּן קָרְאוּ לַיָּמִים הָאֵלֶּה פוּרִים עַל־שֵׁם הַפּוּר עַל־כֵּן עַל־כָּל־
דִּבְרֵי הָאִגֶּרֶת הַזֹּאת וּמָה־רָאוּ עַל־כָּכָה וּמָה הִגִּיעַ אֲלֵיהֶם:

9:26 THEREFORE, THEY [THE JEWS] CALLED THESE DAYS
PURIM AFTER THE WORD *PUR*. FOLLOWING ALL THAT
HAD BEEN WRITTEN IN THIS LETTER AND EVERYTHING
THAT THEIR EYES HAD SEEN, AND EVERYTHING THAT
HAD HAPPENED TO THEM,

This verse is completed by the verse that follows. Still wanting to explain the fixing of
the date for Purim as well as the reason for its celebration, the *Targum* adds to its
translation, following its rendering of *pur*, "that they might observe these days every
year and that they might publicize these days of miracles and that the words of the
M'gillah [Scroll of Esther] might be heard throughout the people of the House of Israel
that all might know why these days of Purim were established and how a miracle
occurred for Mordecai and Esther and how salvation was afforded them."

Since the author notes "this letter," it is natural to assume that those who read the
verse would want to know which letter. Rashi takes "this letter" to indicate that the
holiday was fixed for the Jews of Shushan and for all generations. He says that "what
their eyes had seen" is a reference to the participants and what was done. Rashi also
understands "what had happened to them" to refer to a number of things recorded
in the Book of Esther (as elaborated in the *Targum* and midrash) that the participants
in the narrative only understand after the events described in the narrative have
concluded: the original feast (which had precipitated the events in the book); why
Ahasuerus made profane use of some of the sacred vessels of the Temple and what
happened as a result; how Satan came to dance among them and kill Vashti; why
Haman became envious of Mordecai and what happened to him (namely, that he
and his sons were hanged); why Mordecai would not bow down to Haman; and why
Esther invited Haman.

ט:כז קִיְּמוּ וְקִבְּלוּ הַיְּהוּדִים עֲלֵיהֶם וְעַל־זַרְעָם וְעַל כָּל־הַנִּלְוִים עֲלֵיהֶם
וְלֹא יַעֲבוֹר לִהְיוֹת עֹשִׂים אֵת שְׁנֵי הַיָּמִים הָאֵלֶּה כִּכְתָבָם וְכִזְמַנָּם
בְּכָל־שָׁנָה וְשָׁנָה:

9:27 THE JEWS COMMITTED THEMSELVES AND THEIR
CHILDREN AND THOSE WHO MIGHT JOIN THEM TO
OBSERVE WITHOUT FAIL, EACH AND EVERY YEAR, THESE
TWO DAYS IN THE PRESCRIBED MANNER AND AT THE
CORRECT TIME.

This verse records the willingness of the ancient Persian Jewish community to observe Purim. By virtue of their commitment, subsequent generations are also obligated to observe Purim. The *Targum* adds to its translation the way in which Purim is to be observed: Jews are to read *M'gillat Esther* in their synagogues from the eleventh to the fifteenth of the month, depending upon whether they live in walled or open cities.

Rashi understands "those who might join them" as converts to Judaism. We would argue that they don't necessarily have to be converts. It is a reference to anyone who casts their lot (pun intended) with the Jewish people and makes the choice to join them in their observance of the festival of Purim. Nevertheless, he wants us to understand that the celebration of Purim should be undertaken in a specific way. Thus, he takes *kichtavam*, which we translate as "prescribed manner," literally, "according to its writing," and understands it to mean the Scroll of Esther, the *M'gillah*, to be written in *k'tav ashurit*, literally, "the Assyrian script," that is, in Aramaic script.

Ibn Ezra agrees with Rashi's notion that "those who might join" is a reference to converts to Judaism. He understands "without fail" to mean that every Jew must observe Purim. Because it is not a minor festival, the ritual practices of Purim must be specifically observed. For Ibn Ezra, "every year" means that Purim is to be observed during both regular and leap years.

ט:כח וְהַיָּמִים הָאֵלֶּה נִזְכָּרִים וְנַעֲשִׂים בְּכָל־דּוֹר וָדוֹר מִשְׁפָּחָה וּמִשְׁפָּחָה
מְדִינָה וּמְדִינָה וְעִיר וָעִיר וִימֵי הַפּוּרִים הָאֵלֶּה לֹא יַעַבְרוּ מִתּוֹךְ
הַיְּהוּדִים וְזִכְרָם לֹא יָסוּף מִזַּרְעָם:

9:28 THESE DAYS ARE TO BE REMEMBERED AND OBSERVED IN
EVERY GENERATION AND BY EVERY FAMILY IN EVERY
PROVINCE AND IN EVERY CITY SO THAT THESE DAYS OF
PURIM SHALL NEVER CEASE AMONG THE JEWS NOR
THEIR MEMORY END AMONG THEIR CHILDREN.

The importance of the story of Esther and its annual retelling during the celebration of Purim is made clear by the author. Further evidence for its import is found in the Talmud (*M'gillah* 6b) and Maimonides (*Hilchot M'gillah* 2:18), where we are reminded that Purim will be the only holiday celebrated during the messianic era. The *Targum* specifies the manner and observance and those observing: Purim is to be observed with feasts and by all members of the House of Israel, priests, Levites, and Israelites; in this manner and by such Jews, Purim will be preserved among the Jews of all generations.

Rashi explains that "days...be remembered" refers to the reading of the *M'gillah* and that the days "observed" refers to feasts, rejoicing, and the sending of gifts. He understands "every family" to mean that people are to gather together, eat and drink together, so that the days of Purim may never be forgotten. He takes "their memory" to refer to the reading of the *M'gillah*.

Ibn Ezra emphasizes that "these days are to be remembered and observed 'by every family in every province'" so that no one should think that just because there may be no other Jew in a particular place or one has moved to a new province that one is free from the obligation of observing Purim. He thinks that *yasuf* does mean "end," but he thinks that it is derived from a two-letter Hebrew root (*samech-peh*). He argues that the Jews did observe Purim but ceased doing so after a time. It is for that reason, as suggested in 9:29 and 9:31, that Esther had to confirm Mordecai's enactment of the holiday.

ט:כט וַתִּכְתֹּב אֶסְתֵּר הַמַּלְכָּה בַת־אֲבִיחַיִל וּמָרְדֳּכַי הַיְּהוּדִי אֶת־כָּל־
תֹּקֶף לְקַיֵּם אֵת אִגֶּרֶת הַפֻּרִים הַזֹּאת הַשֵּׁנִית:

9:29 QUEEN ESTHER, DAUGHTER OF ABIHAIL, WROTE A
SECOND LETTER CONCERNING PURIM, CONFIRMING
WITH FULL AUTHORITY THAT IT WAS WRITTEN BY
MORDECAI.

This is the letter that is referenced in the previous verse. The *Targum* follows its translation of "authority" with the word *d'nisa* (of a miracle). While Rashi agrees with the *Targum*'s assessment that the Esther story is indeed a miracle, he suggests that there was a series of different miracles that involved Ahasuerus, Haman, Esther, and Mordecai. For him, the second letter refers to what occurred the following year (even if it doesn't make sense that the book could both present what should be done and record what had been done at the same time). According to Rashi, messages were sent the following year to remind the Jews of Persia to observe Purim. Ibn Ezra contends that the second letter was written by both Esther and Mordecai to confirm that the first one was written by Mordecai.

ט:ל וַיִּשְׁלַח סְפָרִים אֶל־כָּל־הַיְּהוּדִים אֶל־שֶׁבַע וְעֶשְׂרִים וּמֵאָה מְדִינָה
מַלְכוּת אֲחַשְׁוֵרוֹשׁ דִּבְרֵי שָׁלוֹם וֶאֱמֶת:

9:30 HE [MORDECAI] SENT MESSAGES TO ALL THE JEWS IN
THE 127 PROVINCES OF THE KINGDOM OF AHASUERUS:
WORDS OF ASSURANCE AND COMFORT.

While it is not specified who sends the messages, we assume that it is Mordecai because Esther and Mordecai are the subjects of the previous verses. The king could have offered the message—he certainly had the power to do so—but it seems unlikely. The king did not previously communicate directly with the Jewish community—and presumably has no real relationship with it. Nor would readers assume from the character portrait painted throughout the book by the author that he would be motivated to do so.

The last phrase in the verse is *shalom ve-emet* (literally, ''peace and truth''), which we understand as a colloquial expression for good wishes. The *Targum* offers little additional insight as it translates *shalom* as *sh'lama* (''perfection, soundness, health, and peace,'' according to Jastrow, p. 1586). The second word, *emet*, is translated by the *Targum* as *heim'nuta* (''trust, confidence, and faith,'' according to Jastrow, p. 347). According to Ibn Ezra, ''peace'' comes to the Jews because they have fulfilled the mitzvot and therefore do not have to fear being punished by God. The word *emet* (truth) indicates that the Jews are obligated to observe Purim because they made a commitment to do so (in 9:27).

ט:לא לְקַיֵּם אֶת־יְמֵי הַפֻּרִים הָאֵלֶּה בִּזְמַנֵּיהֶם כַּאֲשֶׁר קִיַּם עֲלֵיהֶם מָרְדֳּכַי הַיְּהוּדִי וְאֶסְתֵּר הַמַּלְכָּה וְכַאֲשֶׁר קִיְּמוּ עַל־נַפְשָׁם וְעַל־זַרְעָם דִּבְרֵי הַצּוֹמוֹת וְזַעֲקָתָם:

9:31 THESE DAYS OF PURIM ARE TO BE OBSERVED AT THEIR PROPER TIMES AS ESTABLISHED BY MORDECAI THE JEW AND ESTHER THE QUEEN, AS THEY [THE JEWS] HAD COMMITTED THEMSELVES AND THEIR CHILDREN TO DO SO IN REGARD TO FASTS AND RELATED LAMENTATIONS.

This verse is included to make sure that Purim is observed by the Jewish community of the future. The observance of Purim is described as one of the many obligations of being a Jew. Moreover, Jews have a responsibility to observe Purim because their ancestors made a commitment to do so on their behalf.

Anticipating that readers may wonder about when to celebrate Purim during a leap year, the *Targum* adds that the celebration will be in Adar II during leap years. Ibn Ezra uses the verse to teach us a little about Jewish history and sectarianism. He suggests that most people might think that the phrase ''had committed themselves'' is a reference to the Fast of Esther. Others, such as the Karaites, think that it refers to the three days of fasting in the month of Nisan. Ibn Ezra thinks that the phrase refers to the fasts that are described in the Book of Zechariah (which occur in Tammuz, Av, Tishrei, and Tevet, and which are ''...to be to the House of Judah, joy and gladness and cheerful seasons'' [Zechariah 8:19]), which he takes to mean the festival of Purim.

He explains that the phrase "related lamentations" is relevant to the fasting. Jews would pray and cry out to God during the fast. The same phrase "truth and peace" also concludes the selected verse from Zechariah, which might have motivated Ibn Ezra to find his explanation of this verse there.

ט:לב וּמַאֲמַר אֶסְתֵּר קִיַּם דִּבְרֵי הַפֻּרִים הָאֵלֶּה וְנִכְתָּב בַּסֵּפֶר:

9:32 ESTHER'S ORDER, CONFIRMING THE REGULATIONS OF PURIM, WAS WRITTEN DOWN IN THE RECORD.

The *Targum* adds *v'al y'doi d'mord'chai* (on the hands of Mordecai) after its translation of "Esther's order" to make sure that readers understand that Mordecai played a role in shaping these regulations. Like the *Targum*, Rashi is not comfortable with the idea that a woman, even Queen Esther, could establish something that Jews would be required to do. So Rashi writes that "Esther requested that the scholars of the generation establish this and write it down along with the other books." Ibn Ezra laments that this book, the one in which these regulations were written down, was lost along with other books in Jewish history.

Mishlo-ach Manot

Sometimes called *shalachmanos* (in Yiddish and in Ashkenazi Hebrew), *mishlo-ach manot* refers to the gifts required to be sent to friends to fulfill one of the three primary Purim mitzvot. During the day on Purim, one must send at least two (different) items of ready-to-eat food to at least one person. However, many people send out packages to many people just prior to the festival. Some people use the opportunity of sending these gift baskets to repair broken relationships.

Leap Years

Because the Jewish calendar is a soli-lunar calendar (guided by the moon and corrected by the seasons of the sun), its leap year includes an extra month. (It is similar to the Chinese calendar in this regard.) Because of the difference of eleven days between twelve lunar months and one solar year, the calendar contains an extra lunar month once every two or three years, for a total of seven times in every nineteen-year cycle. Leap years, which contain thirteen months (Adar II is the extra month), are the third, sixth, eighth, eleventh, fourteenth, seventeenth, and nineteenth years of the cycle.

Gifts to the Poor

Some consider the mitzvah of giving gifts to the poor (*matanot la-evyonim*) to be the most important of Purim. Such gifts can be either monetary or provisions of food—not to be confused with or fulfilled by the giving of *mishlo-ach manot*.

Fast of Esther

The Fast of Esther, on the thirteenth of Adar, is observed to reflect the fast observed by Mordecai, Esther, and the ancient Persian Jewish community on the day on which Haman was to destroy the Jewish community. Instead, the Jewish community destroyed its enemies. The Jewish community fasted in the face of an impending war. This fast is named for Esther because she was the one who first requested it (Esther 4:16).

In the text, the fast is three days long. Today it is not observed for three days, nor is it observed on any of the original dates (14–16 Nisan). (Fasting is not permitted in Nisan—except for the fast of the firstborn prior to Passover—because it is the month in which the redemption from Egypt took place.). Today's fast is in memory of the fast observed by the Jewish community on the day of their mobilization for fighting against their enemies. Nevertheless, it is called by the name of Esther since it was she who first proposed its observance. There is a practice among some Jews to fast for three days—on the Monday, Thursday, and Monday after Purim. Others choose to fast on the night of

13 Adar as well as on the day of 13 Adar, since the original fast was observed night and day. Nevertheless, since this fast is not mentioned in any of the prophetic writings, its guiding rules are considerably more lenient than those for other fast days.

Karaites

Karaite Judaism or Karaism is a Jewish sectarian group characterized by its acceptance of the Written Torah and a rejection of the Oral Law, that is, Rabbinic Judaism, which the Karaites deemed inauthentic. Thus, its practices are derived from the Torah and not from the Rabbinic writings of the Mishnah and Talmud. The word "Karaite" emerges from the Hebrew word for "readers (of Scripture)." At one time, the Karaites represented a significant population. Today, they represent approximately two thousand members in the United States, about one hundred families in Istanbul, and twelve thousand in Israel, mostly living near the town of Ramle.

Some common practices of the Karaites, different from the rest of Judaism, include determining of the beginning of the new year based on the ripening of the barley crop in the Land of Israel, since such instructions are included in the Torah. They do not put mezuzot on their doorposts nor do they wear *t'fillin*, and they eat milk and meat together.

GLEANINGS

Hamantaschen

A hamantasch is not a "Haman's pocket" (or "Haman's ear") as most of us were once taught in Hebrew school, but a German-derived *"mohn"* (poppyseed) *"tasch"* (pocket). Okay, that's straightforward—but why do we eat them on Purim of all times, a pre-spring, full-moon festival? Why not Sukkos or Tu b'Shvat?

What is a hamantasch? A sacred vulva filled with black seeds. A food, source of nourishment, which we make with our hands reflecting our (women's) felt sense of self-containment, of creativity, and generativity.

Ancient images of goddesses reveal that certain parts of the body—breasts, vulva, belly, buttocks—were believed to be holy, combining biological function with processes of spiritual transformation. Hamantaschen remind us that the image of the female body was humanity's first conceptualization of the workings of the cosmos. The Earth was a mother, fecund like us. Patriarchal writings speak of women's bodies as "empty vessels"; the hamantasch, however, represents revering our bodies as metaphors for creation.

Therefore...roll 'em, fill 'em, bake 'em, eat 'em, send 'em to friends, eat your friends', let them eat yours, feed 'em to your husband. On the full moon of Adar, the hamantasch, God willing, should not be mistaken for a mere cookie or for Haman's tricorn hat. Hamantaschen are our, and Earth's, bodies, revered as an ultimate metaphor for the divine Creator. They were (and, given the right ritual, could once again be) sacred, representing women's capacity to birth and to nourish, from our own holy bodies.

Susan Schnur, "Tracing the Hamantasch Herstory:
Take Back the Kitchen," *Lilith* 23 (Spring 1998): 1

Nistar b'nistar b'Megillat Esther
[Hidden in Hiddenness in the Book of Esther]

And then—and then—
A Darkness appeared,
Her Head wrapped in mourning,
Her tallit all black,
Her Place only Absence,
Nistar b'nistar:

Her Voice was a Silence:
"I came to defend you,
My people beloved;
I strengthened your hand
to beat back your foes;
But then you betrayed Me.
For your hand became frenzied,
You struck down the innocent,
You struck down my children
While they reached out to Me.

On the day of rejoicing
You hallowed My Name;
In My Own Tree of Life,
You hollowed out life.
You scooped out the juice,
you left only a mockery
A pretense of My Self.

And I see—yes, I see—
That in the days still to come
Your deeds will give warrant
To a child of your children,
To murder your cousins,
The children of Ishmael,
The children of Abraham,

In the Place of his grave,
On this day of rejoicing.

So My Name I withdraw—
Yes, My Name will be hidden,
Nistar b'nistar;

For I will not permit you
to call out from this Scroll
My name on this day.

I have taught you that Purim,
Alone of the seasons,
Will continue beyond
the time of Mashiach.

On the day that both families
of Abraham's offspring
do tshuvah for their murders,
their murders of each other,
on that day will my Name
take its Place in the Megillah.

On that day Purim
and Yom Ha'K'Purim
will at last be one.

On that day, at last,
This Purim will lead you
And light up your way
to the Days of Mashiach.

On that day will My Name
Take Its Place in the Megillah.

Arthur Waskow, *Godwrestling: Round Two*
(Woodstock, VT: Jewish Lights, 1996), 220–21.

Stop Being Marranos

I think the time is ripe for us to stop being Marranos [hidden Jews] and establish our Jewish integrity. That will come when we make the Covenant the basis of our existence, when we link our lives with our people, joining in its historic pact with God. This commitment focuses Jewishness in an act of self—not in ideas, or practice, or birth alone; but all of these now will take their significance from an utterly fundamental relationship of self with God and people. I do not know quite what forms of Jewishness this will lead to. I only know that if one cares, one must act. If we will to be Jews, if we make our Jewishness our means of facing existence, then every part of our lives will be Jewish. Since we are part of a historic tie, we will honor the tradition; and since we affirm this in our being, we will create and innovate so as to express it our way. One cannot know where such personalist covenanting may lead us. But I am less afraid of what we may choose in such Jewish integrity than that we will do nothing and by our indolence perpetuate our Marrano inauthenticity.

Eugene Borowitz, *The Masks Jews Wear: The Self-Deception of American Jewry*
(New York: Simon and Schuster, 1973), 207–8

The Jews' War

Ahashverosh's largesse on this occasion differs from his previous gestures: The king seeks out Esther's behest in the absence of any initiative on her part. Indeed, his words in the Hebrew text are packed into the same verse as Ahashverosh's previous thought—about the numbers of anti-Semites who must have died throughout the empire in the Jews' war—and the association between the two is unmistakable. With visions of blood dancing before his eyes, and afraid as to what may happen next, Ahashverosh's relationship with his Jewish queen undergoes a final, traumatic revision: It is Esther who now embodies power in the king's eyes, and it is he who offers his favors—his *service*—in an effort to gain favor with her. Their relationship is finally and perfectly reversed: Esther, who had come into Ahashverosh's bedchamber five years earlier in search of a way of winning him over so as to avoid a life as a discarded harem girl, now finds the king anxiously seeking to win *her* pleasure.

In this context, it is obvious that Ahashverosh demonstratively (or perhaps unconsciously) drops the hedge, seeking an upper bound on her request of "only" half the kingdom; the implication is that she might now ask for the entire kingdom.

In practice, once it is he who is seeking out her favor, he does not even need to offer all this: It has already been granted. In fact, Esther asks for much less. "If it please the king, let the Jews in Susa do tomorrow according to the law for today, and let Haman's ten sons be hanged on the gallows." (9:13)

Both parts of Esther's answer are straightforward. Like the king she has no way of knowing what has happened in the rest of the empire. In the best case, the war in the provinces will have to come to an end that night with the anti-Semitic menace eradicated; in the worst, the war will have to be extended by a decree from the palace. Her request is that the Jewish reign of arms in Susa be allowed to continue until there is news of what happened in the rest of the empire. The point is that in the capital, at least, the initiative should remain in Mordechai's hands until he is able to determine what should happen next. The Jews are therefore permitted to continue holding the streets of Susa at swordpoint for another twenty-four hours, flushing out of hiding another three hundred of their enemies. Moreover, the bodies of Haman's sons, in life the very symbol of the remainder of anti-Semitic power, are transformed into a symbol of Jewish effectiveness when these grisly relics are put on display for potential opponents to consider.

By the time the streets of Susa have grown quiet after the second day's battle, reports have begun to arrive from the other corners of the kingdom. Everywhere, the victory of the Jews has become a rout. Men have been hounded out and struck down, the spectre of the massacre of which Haman had dreamed is dead, the decree which has hung over the heads of the Jews for so long has been lifted. And the day on which the enemies of the Jews had hoped to rule over them has been transformed, miraculously, into a day of honor and glory, with the Jews themselves achieving rule over those who hated them.

Yoram Hazony, *The Dawn: Political Teachings of the Book of Esther*
(Jerusalem Press: Shalem Press, 1995), 209–10

CHAPTER TEN

י:א וַיָּשֶׂם הַמֶּלֶךְ אֲחַשְׁוֵרוֹשׁ מַס עַל־הָאָרֶץ וְאִיֵּי הַיָּם:

10:1 KING AHASUERUS LEVIED A TAX ON THE LAND AND ON
THE ISLANDS.

The word *mas*, which we translate as "tax," means an extraction of wealth in any
manner from a people by power of any kind. Koehler-Baumgartner translates it as
"forced labor" (p. 603) or "taxes" (p. 604), but it is hard to determine its precise
meaning in this verse. The *Targum* considers it a *carga*—capitation tax, tax, or tribute
(Jastrow, p. 664). The answer may lie in whether Persia had a money or labor
economy during Ahasuerus's reign. In any case, this verse is a difficult ending to the
story. Perhaps the author is attempting to describe business as usual—now that the
crisis is over. Or maybe the author wants to demonstrate that the king has to recoup
his losses following the death of many of his subjects. Ibn Ezra suggests that the king
extracted funds from the people—even from those who did not live on lands under
his authority—because they were afraid of him. And they were afraid of him, argues
Ibn Ezra, because Mordecai was his second-in-command (see 10:3).

י:ב וְכָל־מַעֲשֵׂה תָקְפּוֹ וּגְבוּרָתוֹ וּפָרָשַׁת גְּדֻלַּת מָרְדֳּכַי אֲשֶׁר גִּדְּלוֹ
הַמֶּלֶךְ הֲלוֹא־הֵם כְּתוּבִים עַל־סֵפֶר דִּבְרֵי הַיָּמִים לְמַלְכֵי מָדַי
וּפָרָס:

10:2 ALL HIS MIGHTY AND POWERFUL ACTS AND THE
DETAILING OF THE KING'S RAISING OF MORDECAI TO
GREATNESS ARE RECORDED IN THE CHRONICLES OF THE
KINGS OF MEDIA AND PERSIA.

These books are not extant, if in fact they ever existed.

יֹ:ג כִּי מָרְדֳּכַי הַיְּהוּדִי מִשְׁנֶה לַמֶּלֶךְ אֲחַשְׁוֵרוֹשׁ וְגָדוֹל לַיְּהוּדִים וְרָצוּי
לְרֹב אֶחָיו דֹּרֵשׁ טוֹב לְעַמּוֹ וְדֹבֵר שָׁלוֹם לְכָל־זַרְעוֹ:

10:3 So Mordecai the Jew ranked next to the king. He was a most important Jew, well-regarded by most of his brethren, looking out for his people's benefit, and speaking out on behalf of the welfare of his community.

Here is more praise heaped on Mordecai and more acknowledgment of his powerful role. The *Targum* adds that Mordecai was *gizbara v'sava* (the commander and the elder of his people) and that his fame had reached from one end of the earth to the other, so that all the kings feared him and trembled when they mentioned his name. Mordecai, the *Targum* continues, resembled a brilliant star circling among the stars like the brightness of dawn. He was the leader of the Jews.

Rashi tells us why he was so well-regarded by other Jews but not the entire Jewish community. Some of the members of the Sanhedrin turned away from him because he became *karov lamalchut* (a member of the royal court). This caused him to neglect his study of Torah. We follow Rashi in his explanation of *zaro* (literally "his seed")— which we translate as "community"—as a reference to Mordecai's people, not just his own family. It is clear that the commentators are not comfortable with Mordecai's new renown, especially because he gained it through fear. Nevertheless, Ibn Ezra simply tells us that Mordecai didn't find favor with all the people because they were jealous of him. No one can please everybody.

Ibn Ezra plays on the word *doreish* (literally "seeking," which we translate as "looking out for"). It would have been enough had Mordecai done good for anyone who would have asked (*doreish*) him. However, Mordecai sought to do good without being asked. Then Ibn Ezra goes on to explain that *zaro* refers to Mordecai's children and grandchildren. In a statement that perhaps comes from his personal experience, Ibn Ezra notes that children fear their parents. But Mordecai sought the welfare of his children even though they were under his control. How much more so would he have done it for his people! (As fathers, we think that Ibn Ezra's logic is backwards.

If he does it for his people, then certainly he would do it for his children—who should always come first.) Finally, Ibn Ezra thinks that Scripture indicates Mordecai's greatness and humility, just as it does with Moses in the following words: "Now Moses was a very humble man, more so than any human being on earth" (Numbers 12:3).

GLEANINGS

Esther as Historical Romance

The Book of Esther tells a story, and tells it so well that few modern students of the Bible incline to regard it as a record of fact—it reads so much like literary fiction. And, indeed, the incidents related are so deftly knit together, and the characters portrayed are so artistically drawn, that no reader can fail to be impressed with the superb craftsmanship of the narrator of the story.

Yet the manner in which a story is told has no real bearing on the nature of the facts related. The historian aims to do more than transcribe recorded events; he strives to depict the conditions and forces that produced the events, as well as the principal personalities that determined their course. And in molding the material, he not infrequently displays the skill of the literary artist. . . .

There is nothing in our story, beyond some minor details, that is in direct conflict with the known facts of recorded history. The central theme of the book, the cruel design of Haman to destroy the Jews and the successful intervention of Esther and Mordecai, is not so hard to accept that it must be rejected as untrue. In the light of present-day events, it is not quite safe to discredit the incredible. We think it therefore more reasonable to regard the Book of Esther as a species of historical romance than as a work of pure fiction.

Israel Bettan, *The Five Scrolls*
(Cincinnati: Union of American Hebrew Congregations, 1950), 195, 199

The Depths of Depravity

We now know the depths of depravity to which the human species can descend. The range of human possibility, the depth of evil revealed by the Nazis, goes beyond anything previously imagined. Indeed, the inability to imagine anything so horrible limited the victims' ability to defend themselves.

The Nazis attacked the Jew to fundamentally transform the meaning of what it was to be human—to create a master race—and they succeeded, achieving the opposite. Having surveyed the human depravity demonstrated by the Nazis, we can never again relate to our own humanity in the same way: we can never trust ourselves; we must inevitably think less of ourselves. Some may assimilate this knowledge easily, but it is no wonder that a person who experienced the horror, having seen what life had turned into, would choose to stay with the dead. . . .

Humanity had been undone.

Edward Feld, *The Spirit of Renewal: Crisis and Response in Jewish Life*
(Woodstock, VT: Jewish Lights Publishing, 1991), 93–94

A Kavanah *Meditation for Purim*

Purim can be seen as the celebration that ends our yearly holiday cycle. We begin with *Pesach*, when it is the present and mighty hand of God alone that saves us. We end the year with *Purim*, when God's self is actually "hidden," masked within the human story of our ancestors. We must enact salvation for ourselves from ourselves. *Ad-lo-yadah*, another meaning: "until you don't know" . . . has a higher degree of consciousness. It is a messianic/mystical moment when there is *no* difference between Haman and Mordecai, good and evil, for both are found in the Holy One, "who created light and darkness, made peace and created evil."

Temple Beth El of the Sudbury River Valley (Massachusetts)

Happiness

According to the Hebrew calendar, which uses the seasons to balance the progress of time marked by the moon, the month of Adar (around February-March) is ushered in by unmitigated joy. This attitude is generally ascribed to the spirit of Purim that shapes the entire month. So, through the frivolous celebration of the festival of Purim, we turn everything in our religious life upside down and inside out. The festive meal that we expect to usher in a holiday is held at the end of the festival rather than at the beginning of it. And we put on masks that allow us for a short period of time to pretend to be someone else and, at the same time, take ourselves less seriously. Even the teachers whose words we usually respect are subject to loving ridicule. Having survived the challenge of Haman, we are thrilled just to be alive.

We are also nearing the end of winter and the beginning of spring. For similar reasons, such change helps to raise the spirit. We get just a hint of what is around the corner: singing birds, blossoming flowers, and the buzz of neighborhood lawn mowers. Just the refreshing breath of fresh air reminds us of how lucky we are to be alive. So, maybe tonight we should work a little less and play a little more. There will be more time to do our work tomorrow.

Kerry M. Olitzky and Lori Forman, *Restful Reflections:*
Nighttime Inspiration to Calm the Soul, Based on Jewish Wisdom
(Woodstock, VT: Jewish Lights Publishing, 2001), 89

Esther as the Dawn

Esther is the dawn because that light which comes to the Jews comes from her, of her own creation and her own power. Neither the seething firmament of the old Jewish night, nor the astrological fatalism of idolaters like Haman casting their lots, will now be the final arbiter of events; for Esther is herself a star, if only she wills it, a sun in her own right.

Yoram Hazony, *The Dawn: Political Teachings in the Book of Esther*
(Jerusalem: Shalem Press, 1995), 248

Bibliography

Berlin, Adele. *The JPS Bible Commentary: Esther.* Philadelphia: Jewish Publication Society, 2003.

Bronner, Leila Leah. *From Eve to Esther: Rabbinic Reconstructions of Biblical Women.* Gender and the Biblical Tradition. Louisville, KY: Westminster/John Knox Press, 1994.

Fox, Michael V. *Character and Ideology in the Book of Esther.* 2nd ed. Grand Rapids, MI: W.B. Eerdmans, 2001.

Glaser, Connie, and Barbara Smaley. *What Queen Esther Knew: Business Strategies from a Biblical Sage.* Emmaus, PA: Rodale Press, 2003.

Hazony, Yoram. *The Dawn: Political Teachings in the Book of Esther.* Jerusalem: Shalem Press, 1995.

Horowitz, Elliot. *Reckless Rites: Purim and the Legacy of Jewish Violence.* Jews, Christians, and Muslims from the Ancient to the Modern World. Princeton: Princeton University Press, 2006.

Jastrow, Marcus. *A Dictionary of the Targumim, the Talmud Babli and Yerushalmi, and the Midrashic Literature.* New York: Judaica Press, 2004.

Waldman, J. T. *Megillat Esther.* Philadelphia: Jewish Publication Society, 2005.

Biographies

Rachel Adler is associate professor of Modern Jewish Thought and Judaism and Gender at the School of Religion, University of Southern California, and the Rabbinical School at Hebrew Union College–Jewish Institute of Religion, Los Angeles. Dr. Adler was one of the first theologians to integrate feminist perspectives and concerns into the interpretation of Jewish texts and the renewal of Jewish law and ethics. She is the author of many articles that have appeared in *Blackwell's Companion to Feminist Philosophy, Beginning Anew: A Woman's Companion to the High Holy Days, Contemporary Jewish Religious Thought, Lifecycles, The Jewish Condition,* and *On Being a Jewish Feminist.*

Israel Bettan was a rabbi and professor of rabbinics and homiletics at Hebrew Union College–Jewish Institute of Religion. His unique style of teaching continues to influence the way rabbinics and homiletics are taught to rabbinic students at HUC-JIR.

Eugene B. Borowitz is the Sigmund L. Falk Distinguished Professor of Education and Jewish Religious Thought at Hebrew Union College–Jewish Institute of Religion, where he has taught since 1962. Dr. Borowitz is the author of numerous books, including *Renewing the Covenant*, and the first person to receive a National Foundation for Jewish Culture Achievement Award in Scholarship for work in the field of Jewish thought.

Aliza Bulow is program director for the Jewish Experience in Denver, Colorado.

Tamara Cohen is a Jewish feminist writer, activist, and educator. She currently works as the director of Lesbian, Gay, Bisexual and Transgender Affairs at the University of Florida and as the spiritual leader of the Greater Washington Coalition for Jewish Life in western Connecticut.

Wayne Dosick is a rabbi and the spiritual guide of the Elijah Minyan in San Diego and adjunct professor of Jewish Studies at the University of San Diego. He is the author of *Golden Rules, Dancing with God,* and *When Life Hurts.*

David Ellenson is president of Hebrew Union College–Jewish Institute of Religion, where he is also the I. H. and Anna Grancell Professor of Jewish Religious Thought. Dr. Ellenson is the author of numerous books, articles, and monographs, including *Tradition in Transition: Orthodoxy, Halakhah and the Boundaries of Modern Jewish Identity*; *Rabbi Esriel Hildesheimer and the Creation of a Modern Jewish Orthodoxy*; and *Between Tradition and Culture: The Dialectics of Jewish Religion and Identity in the Modern World*.

Edward Feld was Jewish chaplain and Hillel director at Princeton University for twenty years before serving as rabbi of the Society for the Advancement of Judaism in New York City. Rabbi Feld has been a Senior Fellow at the Shalom Hartman Institute in Jerusalem, where he was organizer of its theology seminar. He also served as the rabbi-in-residence at the Jewish Theological Seminary of America, located in New York City.

Lori Forman is the senior vice principal, curriculum and administration, at the Bergen High School for Jewish Studies. Ordained by the Jewish Theological Seminary in 1988, Rabbi Forman was a member of the first JTS rabbinical school class to include women.

Herbert A. Friedman served as rabbi at Temple Emanuel in Denver, as an army chaplain, as CEO of the United Jewish Appeal, and as the founding president of the Wexner Heritage Program. Rabbi Friedman was credited with initiating the Federation system's missions program to Israel, as well as its model of Young Leadership.

Irving ("Yitz") Greenberg is the former president of Jewish Life Network and the founder of CLAL: National Jewish Center for Learning and Leadership. Rabbi Greenberg is also former chair of the United States Holocaust Memorial Council, appointed by President Bill Clinton.

Lauren Grodstein is the author of essays, stories, and reviews, as well as the short story collection *The Best of Animals* and the novel *Reproduction Is the Flaw of Love*. She teaches creative writing at Rutgers University.

David Hartman is founder and co-director of the Shalom Hartman Institute in Jerusalem. He also is professor of Jewish Thought at Hebrew University of Jerusalem. He was the spiritual leader of Congregation Tiferet Beit David Jerusalem in Montreal for many years before moving to Israel. Rabbi Hartman served as an advisor to Zevulun Hammer, former Israeli Minister of Education (1977–1984) and has been advisor to a number of Israeli prime ministers on the subject of religious pluralism in Israel and the relationship between Israel and the Diaspora. Hartman's publications in Jewish philosophy have received wide recognition and become standard references in academic scholarship. He was awarded the National Jewish Book Award in 1977 for *Maimonides: Torah and Philosophic Quest*. In 1993, the Hebrew translation of *A Living Covenant from Sinai to Zion* was awarded the Leah Goldberg Prize. Professor Hartman was awarded the AVI CHAI Prize in 2000, and on the twenty-fifth anniversary of the Shalom Hartman Institute, he was awarded the Guardian of Jerusalem Prize. In 2004 David Hartman was awarded the Samuel Rothberg Prize for Jewish Education by the Hebrew University of Jerusalem.

Yoram Hazony is the founder and provost of the Shalem Center in Jerusalem, where he is presently a director of the Institute for Philosophy, Politics and Religion and a Senior Fellow. He is the author of *The Jewish State: The Struggle for Israel's Soul*. His articles on Judaism, Zionism, and Israel have appeared in various publications, including *The New Republic*, *Commentary*, *The Weekly Standard*, and *Azure*.

Daniel Judson is the director of professional development and placement at the Rabbinical School of Hebrew College in Newton, Massachusetts, and a doctoral candidate in Jewish history at Brandeis University. He served as rabbi of Temple Beth David of the South Shore in Canton, Massachusetts, for ten years and is the co-author of several publications, including *The Rituals and Practices of Jewish Life* and *The Jewish Pregnancy Book*.

Lawrence Kushner is the scholar-in-residence at Congregation Emanu-El in San Francisco and visiting professor of Jewish Spirituality at the Graduate Theological University in Berkeley. Most recently, he was rabbi-in-residence at Hebrew Union College–Jewish Institute of Religion, New York. Rabbi Kushner served as spiritual leader of Congregation Beth El of Sudbury, Massachusetts, for twenty-five years and is the author of numerous books and articles, including *God Was in This Place and I, i Did Not Know*.

Steven Leder is senior rabbi of Wilshire Boulevard Temple in Los Angeles, where he has served since 1986. Rabbi Leder also teaches homiletics at Hebrew Union College–Jewish Institute of Religion, Los Angeles.

Emily Nepon was founding director of the Self-Education Foundation and program director of the Shalom Center.

Vanessa L. Ochs is an associate professor in the department of religious studies at the University of Virginia. She has written several books, including *Inventing Jewish Ritual*, *Sarah Laughed*, and *Words on Fire: One Woman's Journey into the Sacred*.

167

Susan Schnur is a rabbi, writer, and clinical psychologist and serves as editor-at-large for *Lilith Magazine*.

Frederick Schwartz is the resident scholar at Temple Sholom in Chicago, Illinois, having served as its senior rabbi from 1974 to 1997. Rabbi Schwartz has published in Jewish periodicals on such topics as revelation, law, anti-Semitism, history, Martin Buber, and education. He is co-editor of *Essays in Honor of Dr. Freehof*, a volume devoted to writings of Rabbi Solomon B. Freehof of Pittsburgh, with whom Rabbi Schwartz trained.

Brian Strauss is a rabbi at Congregation Beth Yeshurun in Houston, Texas.

Elizabeth Swados is a playwright living in New York City who often explores themes of Jewish identity and feminism in her work.

Jon-Jay Tilsen is rabbi of Congregation Beth El-Keser Israel in New Haven, Connecticut.

Andrew Vogel is rabbi of Temple Sinai in Brookline, Massachusetts. He is well-known for the melody that accompanies the text *Mitzvah goreret mitzvah*, which was the winner of the North American Federation of Temple Youth (NFTY) song competition when he was a youth.

Arthur Waskow is a leader of the Jewish Renewal movement and well-known for his *Freedom Seder*, written following the riots in Washington, D.C., that emerged after the assassination of Dr. Martin Luther King, Jr. The founder and director of the Shalom Center, Rabbi Waskow is the editor of its *New Menorah* journal as well as the author of *Godwrestling* and *Down-to-Earth Judaism*.

Elizabeth Wurtzel is a writer, best known for her provocative work *Prozac Nation*.

David Zauderer is a rabbi and member of the Atlanta Scholars Kollel and a staff writer for *Torah from Dixie*.

TABLE DES MATIÈRES

Imprimerie de la manutention à Mayenne (France) - Octobre 2011 - N° 768850F

Dépot légal : 4ᵉ trimestre 2011